D1209721

ELIZABETHAN ACTING

BY

B. L. JOSEPH

OXFORD UNIVERSITY PRESS
LONDON : GEOFFREY CUMBERLEGE
1951

Oxford University Press, Amen House, London E.C. 4

GLASGOW NEW YORK TORONTO MELBOURNE WELLINGTON
BOMBAY CALCUTTA MADRAS CAPE TOWN

Geoffrey Cumberlege, Publisher to the University

PREFACE

THE spelling of my sources has been maintained in quotation; but contractions have been expanded except for the ampersand. For major quotations from Shakespeare the text of the First Folio (1623) has been used: where it has been necessary to quote from one or other of the Quartos, the fact is noted.

It is simple to acknowledge the help received in writing this book; difficult to convey accurately the quality of my debt both to individuals and institutions. My first encouragement came from Professor E. C. Llewellyn of the University College of South Wales and Monmouthshire, to the Librarian of which, Mr. S. O. Moffet, and his Staff I owe more than they perhaps realize. During the early stages of this work I was guided and encouraged by Mr. Nevill Coghill. Later I have benefited from the comment and encouragement of Professor C. M. Bowra, Mr. J. B. Bamborough, Dr. Percy Simpson, Professor Lord David Cecil, and Professor J. R. R. Tolkien.

I have been fortunate enough to be able to understand from personal experience why so many prefaces bear witness to the help and kindness of the Staff of the Bodleian Library, of Mr. Strickland Gibson, Dr. Hunt, and Dr. Hassall.

I must emphasize the nature of my debt to Professor F. P. Wilson. I have benefited from his suggestions, and from his calling my attention to facts which I am confident I should otherwise have continued to overlook.

It is to the generosity of the University of Wales that I owe the leisure necessary for that large part of the work done during my tenure of a Fellowship.

UNIVERSITY OF BRISTOL   B. L. J.
April 1950

CONTENTS

NOTE

The illustrations of rhetorical gestures of the hand have been taken from John Bulwer's *Chirologia* and *Chironomia* (1644).

I
ACTING AND RHETORIC

THE sources on which I rely for this account of Elizabethan acting are not new in the sense that they are newly
discovered. They have not been lying for centuries hidden
and unknown in the dust of libraries: they have been known and
they have been read, but for a long time it has not been realized
that they contain information which enables us to recapture
much of the atmosphere and many of the details of Elizabethan
stage-playing. Superficially, the works which I am using do not
even appear to be concerned with the stage; they describe the
art of rhetorical delivery, as it was taught to the schoolboys, and
practised by the lawyers, divines, and public speakers of renaissance England. According to sixteenth-century and seventeenth-century writings, however, stage-playing and rhetorical
delivery were so alike, that whoever knows to-day exactly what
was taught to the renaissance orator cannot be far from knowing at
the same time what was done by the actor on the Elizabethan stage.

That what applied to acting in oratory applied also to acting
on the stage is evident in the description of *An Excellent Actor*,
one of the collection of *New and Choice Characters of several
Authors*, which appeared under the name of Sir Thomas Over-
bury in 1615. This character, attributed by some authorities to
John Webster, states categorically: 'Whatsoever is commendable to the grave Orator, is most exquisitely perfect in him; for
by a full and significant action of body, he charmes our attention.'[1] A similar reference to the close connexion between stage-
acting and rhetorical delivery is made by Richard Flecknoe in
his *Short Discourse of the English Stage* (1664). He tells us that
Shakespeare's actor, Richard Burbage, 'had all the parts of an
excellent Orator, (animating his words with speaking, and
Speech with Action).'[2] And covering the same ground a year

[1] *New and Choice Characters* (1615), 6th ed., p. 147.
[2] *A Short Discourse of the English Stage* (1664), sig. G7r.

later, Flecknoe gave a description of the ideal actor in his collection entitled *Aenigmatical Characters*:

There is as much difference betwixt him and a common Actor, as
betwixt a Ballad-singer and an excellent Musician; t'one onely
mouthing it, whilst t'other artfully varies and modulates his voice;
knowing all his graces, even to how much breath he is to give to every
syllable. He has all the parts of an excellent Orator, (animating his
words with speaking, and speech with action) his Auditors being
never more delighted then when he speaks; nor more sorry then
when he holds his peace. Yet even then he is an excellent Actor still,
not falling in his part when he has done his speech, but with his looks
and gesture maintaining it still unto the heighth: imagining *age quod
agis* onely spoke to him.[1]

We find the orator's art linked with that of the actor once
more when Francis Bacon, in the essay 'Of Boldness,' refers to
a 'triuiall Grammar Schoole Text, but yet worthy a wise Mans
Consideration'. This is the well-known story of Demosthenes.
When asked '*what was the Chiefe Part of an Oratour?* he
answered, *Action*; what next? *Action*; what next again? *Action*.
He said it that knew it best; . . . a strange thing, that that Part of
an Oratour, which is but superficiall, and rather the vertue of a
Player; should be placed so high.'[2]

What these writers understood by *Action* is explained by
Thomas Wright in *The Passions of the Mind*.

For action is either a certaine visible eloquence, or an eloquence of
the bodie, or a comely grace in deliuering conceits, or an externall
image of an internall mind, or a shaddow of affections, or three
springs which flow from one fountaine, called *vox, vultus, vita*, voice,
countenance, life. . . . Action then vniuersally is a naturall or artificiall moderation, qualification, modification, or composition of the
voice, countenance, and gesture of the bodie proceeding from some
passion, and apt to stir vp the like.[3]

The fullest account of rhetorical delivery written in English
during the renaissance was the work of John Bulwer, in his
Chirologia and *Chironomia* which appeared together, sharing the

---

[1] *Aenigmatical Characters* (1665), pp. 2–3.
[2] *Essays* (1625), ed. Arber, p. 518.
[3] *The Passions of the Mind* (1604), p. 176.

same title-page, in 1644. Bulwer, who is also known for his pioneer experiments in the education of the deaf and dumb in England, devoted these two treatises to a detailed account of the use of the hand, arm, and fingers in rhetorical delivery. Not content with verbal description, he provided plates illustrating the gestures, thus adding enormously to the value of his work for the modern historian of the Elizabethan stage: they are reproduced in this book. I shall have need to refer to *Chirologia* and *Chironomia* frequently in the following pages, not only because Bulwer gives so many details of what he calls 'manuall rhetoric', but also because he helps to explain the general theory of rhetoric which lay behind the practice of delivery. The cumulative effect of his work, moreover, is such as to convince us that Wright, for instance, was voicing something stronger than a personal opinion when he said that 'in the substance of externall action for the most part oratours and stageplayers agree'. And Wright's advice to orators is that they should 'looke upon other men appassionate. . . . And then leaue the excess and exorbitant leuitie or other defects, and keepe the manner corrected with a prudent mediocritie: and this the best may be marked in stageplaiers, who act excellently.'[1]

During the renaissance, rhetorical delivery was also known as *Pronunciation*. The synonymous usage of *Action* and *Pronunciation* in this respect had its counterpart in Latin, where *actio* and *pronuntiatio* could each be used to denote all that Wright meant by 'voice, countenance, life'. According to Quintilian, this had been the custom in ancient Rome as early as the time of Cicero.[2] Following classical sources, therefore, Sir Thomas Wilson declares that pronunciation is 'an apt ordering, both of the voyce, countenaunce, and al the whole bodie according to the worthinesse of such wordes and matter, as by speech are declared'. And in the next paragraph: 'Pronunciation standeth partly in fashioning the tongue, and partly in framing the iesture.'[3] Similarly,

---

[1] *Ibid.*, p. 179.
[2] *Inst. Orat.* (lib. xi), ed. Butler, iv. 242.
[3] *The Art of Rhetorique* (1560), ed. Mair (1909), p. 218.

Cleon.

Grandiloquentia

Hortensius.

CHI RONO MIA

Andronicus

Deliciæ meæ

Demosthenes.

WM sculp

Roscius.

Cicero.

FIG. 1

the Ramist Abraham Fraunce defines 'vtterance or pronunciation' as 'a fit deliuering of the speach alreadie beautified. It hath
two parts, *Voyce*, and *Gesture*, the one pertaining to the eare,
the other belonging to the eye.'[1]

It is important to note, however, that 'pronunciation' could
also be used in the sense of 'giving utterance', to which we are
accustomed to-day. Wright, for instance, refers to the use of the
voice alone when he says that 'the Rhetoricians likewise doe not
content themselues with the simple pronunciation of their
Orations', adding that they also prescribe rules for gesture.[2] As
in this case, the context usually makes clear in which sense an
Elizabethan is using 'pronunciation'. And even when the meaning is restricted to the use of the voice alone, that, too, could also
be considered as a kind of acting, as we shall see when the
subject is treated more fully later.

Renaissance writers often delighted in suggesting that before
them all had been dark right back to ancient Rome. In their
attachment to the new learning they tended to exaggerate the
shortcomings, both of the middle ages and of their own times.
Thus Vives (1531) attacks contemporary orators because 'nothing
is said in its proper place; their delivery is exaggerated, nothing is
suited to the subject or the occasion, either in the voice, the eyes
or the facial expression, or in the hands and fingers, or in the
movement and bearing of the whole body'.[3] Similarly, in his
well-known attack on contemporary civilization, Cornelius
Agrippa devotes a chapter to the subject *Of Rhetorisme, or of the
Rhetoricall Daunsing*. This, like the rest of his book, is coloured
by the mood of a self-confessed malcontent. Speaking of the
past he declares:

There was moreouer the *Rhetoricall* daunsing, not vnlike that of the
stage players, but not so vehemente, whiche *Socrates, Plato, Cicero,
Quintilian*, and very many of the *Stoickes* thought very profitable,
and necessary for an Oratour: so that it were done with a

[1] *The Arcadian Rhetoric* (1588), sig. I 7^v.
[2] Op. cit., p. 124.
[3] J. L. Vives, *On the Causes of the Corruptions of the Arts* (Bk. IV, Cap. iii),
tr. in unpublished dissertation by Miss R. Stein, Lady Margaret Hall, Oxford.

certayne apt gesture of the bodie, and a setled framing of the countenaunce, and body: and also with the stedfastnesse of the eyes, with the grauity of the countenaunce, with the sounde of the voice applied to euery worde and sentence, with an effectuall mouing of the body to such things, as are expressed, but without greate sturring of the bodie. Yet this daunsing or *Histrionicall* Rhetoricke in the ende began to be lefte of all Oratours . . . and at this presente it is altogyther laid aside: onely it is obserued of some staged Friers (albeit in times paste stage players were banished out of the Churche, and denied the holy Sacrament of Communion) of which some we see at this day to crie out of the pulpit to the people with maruelous strayning of the voyce, with a diuers fashioned countenaunce, with a rolling and wanton eie, with casting abroade of the armes, with daunsing feete, with inflamed reines, and with diuers mouings, reuolutions, turnings aboute, vpward lookes, leapings, gesturing with all his body, as that which bicause of the vnconstancie of the minde is enforced to turne with it: mindefull perhaps of the sentence of *Demosthenes*, who (as it is in *Valerius*) being demaunded, what was the most effectuall in speaking, he answered, Pronunciation.[1]

Sir Thomas Elyot, too, in his denunciation of contemporary public-speaking, complained that the art of 'sterynge of affections of the mynde in this realme was neuer used'. Nevertheless, he grudgingly admits, 'it is to be remembred that in the lernyng of the lawes of this realme, there is at this daye an exercise, wherein is a maner, a shadowe, or figure of the auncient rhetorike'. This was 'the pleadynge used in courte and Chauncery called motes': and as a result of this practice he could bring himself to recognize that, even in his own degenerate day, some lawyers 'pronounce right vehemently'.[2]

There exists, however, a wealth of evidence that the art of 'sterynge of affections of the mynde' in pronunciation had been practised throughout the middle ages, even if not always in exactly the same manner as during the renaissance and in the great days of Greece and Rome. Works on the subject written between the fourth and the tenth centuries are included by

[1] *Of the Vanity and Uncertainty of Arts and Sciences* (1575), sig. I4^v– sig. K^r.
[2] *The Governor* (1531), ed. Foster Watson (1937), pp. 65–6.

Halm in his *Rhetores Latini Minores*.[1] Aelred, abbot of Rievaulx
from 1150 to 1166, complains that the gestures and singing of the
liturgy 'non ad oratorium sed ad theatrum nec ad orandum sed
ad spectandum aestimes convenisse . . . Interim histrionicis qui-
busdam gestibus totum corpus agitatur, torquentur labia, rotant,
ludunt humeri; et ad singulas quasque notas digitorum flexus
respondet'.[2]

Instructions on the art of pronunciation are also to be found
in medieval poetics. In the *Documentum de Arte Versificandi*,
Geoffrey of Vinsauf points out:

Est pronuntiatio quasi totius orationis condimentum, ut sine qua
totum est insipidum et inconditum. Pronuntiatio sic describitur a
Tullio in *Rhetoricis*: 'Pronuntiatio est vocis, vultus, gestus moderatio
cum venustate.' Haec autem tria secum debet habere pronuntiator:
vocem venustam et moderatam, vultum venustum et moderatum,
gestum venustum et moderatum, ne gestus noster sit gestus histrionis
vel operarii, similiter et vox et vultus.

And in the *Poetria Nova*, Chaucer's 'dere mayster soverayn'
treats the subject once more:

> In recitante sonent tres linguae: prima sit oris
> Altera rhetorici vultus, et tertia gestus.[3]

Chaucer himself reminds us that rhetorical delivery was
known to fourteenth-century England. In *The Squire's Tale* the
stranger-knight is thus described:

> He with a manly voys seith his message,
> After the form used in his langage,
> With-outen vyce of sillable or of lettre;
> And, for his tale sholde seme the bettre,
> Accordant to his wordes was his chere,
> As techeth art of speche hem that it lere.[4]

---

[1] C. Halm, *Rhetores Latini Minores* (1863) (seventh-century manuscript),
C. Chirius Fortunatianus, Lib. III, 15–23, *De Pronuntiatione*, pp. 130–4. Sul-
pitius Victor, *De Pronuntiatione* (fourth century), p. 321. C. Julius Victor,
De Pronuntiatione (twelfth-century manuscript), pp. 440–3. Martianus
Capella, *De Rhetorica* (tenth-century manuscript), pp. 484, 485. Karlus Rex
et Albinus Magister, *De Arte Rhetorica Dialogus* (ninth-century manuscript),
pp. 546–7.

[2] *Speculum Charitatis*, ii. 33, ed. Migne; *P.L.* cxcv. 571.

[3] Ed. Faral (1923), pp. 259, 318.   [4] Ed. Skeat (1894), iv. 464.

Again, a passage in Lydgate's *Fall of Princes*, one of the few not based on Boccaccio or de Premierfait, testifies that the sixteenth-century humanists were misinformed about the state of learning some few generations before their own day.

> Pronunciacioun is the fourth armure,
> Necessarie to eueri oratour,
> In such caas whan craft onto nature
> Iioyned is bi dilligent labour
> With execucioun, and that ther be fauour
> In declaryng, with eueri circumstaunce
> Folwyng the mateer in cheer & countenaunce.
>
> An heuy mateer requereth an heuy cheer;
> To a glad mateer longeth weel gladnesse;
> Men in pronouncyng mut folwe the mateer,—
> Old oratours kan bern herof witnesse,—
> A furious compleynt vttrid in distresse:
> This was the maner, as poetis do descryue,
> In his tragedies whan Senec was alyue.
>
> .   .   .   .   .
>
> Thes saide thynges be inli necessarie
> To euery prudent notable oratour,
> Nat to hasti nor ouer long to tarie,
> But to conveie his processe be mesour;
> In cheer accordyng stant al the fauour:
> For in pronouncyng, who lakketh cheer or face,
> Of Tullius scoole stant ferr out of grace.'[1]

Whether they knew or did not know that they had medieval fore-runners, the humanists of the sixteenth century placed much emphasis on the teaching of rhetoric in the English grammar school, and equivalent institutions. As a result, *pronuntiatio* also occupied a prominent place in the curriculum; and this is true of all stages of education. The charters of schools founded during this period usually contain clauses relating to the teaching of rhetorical delivery. It was enjoined in 1544 that the pupils of the grammar and song schools attached to the re-founded Cathedral Church of Worcester should be taught the

[1] Ed. Bergen (1924), iii. 764–5.

correct use of voice and gesture. Chapter Forty of the Articles defines the duties of the Headmaster and Under-master: 'Ambo etiam operam dent, ut discipuli aperte, ornate et distincte, corporis et oris decore servato pronuntiare discant.' A. F. Leach englishes *pronuntiare* as *to speak*; but it is clear that the founders wanted the boys to 'pronounce openly, finely and distinctly, keeping due decorum both with body and with mouth'.[1]

At Winchester, Eton, Westminster, and St. Paul's, as well as in cathedral and grammar schools scattered all over the country, we meet the same insistence, that boys should learn the full rhetorical pronunciation. At Bury St. Edmunds the voice was to be trained even in the lower forms: 'Those who are being instructed in the first elements of grammar are not to utter words at random and without understanding like parrots, but are to pronounce with pleasing and apt modulation, tempered with variety.'[2] And the 1541 charter of King's School, Canterbury, made provision for the teaching of 'due decorum both with their body and their mouth'.[3] No doubt, in his turn, Christopher Marlowe learnt this with the rest.

The importance of rhetorical delivery is also emphasized in works on educational theory. Vives, in *De Tradendis Disciplinis*, demands that 'the exposition of authors should be marked by ease and clearness. In the beginning it should be in the words of the vernacular, and by degrees proceed to Latin, pronounced distinctly and with gestures which may help intelligence, as long as they do not degenerate into the theatrical.'[4]

When Elyot complained that rhetorical delivery was neglected among his contemporaries, he expressed at the same time a hope that young noblemen studying law might be taught the correct use of voice and body:

and verily I suppose, if there mought ones happen some man, hauyng an excellent wytte, to be brought up in suche fourme as I haue

---

[1] *Documents Illustrating Early Education in Worcester*, pp. 132, 145.

[2] *Vide* T. W. Baldwin, *William Shakespere's Small Latine & Lesse Greeke*, i. 301.

[3] A. F. Leach, *Educational Charters*, p. 467.

[4] Tr. Foster Watson, *Vives on Education*, p. 104.

hytherto written, and maye also be exactly or depely lerned in the arte of an Oratour, and also in the lawes of this realme, the Prince so willyng and therto assistinge, undoughtedly it shulde nat be impossible for hym to bring the pleadyng and reasonyng of the lawe, to the auncient forme of noble oratours; and the lawes and exercise thereof beyng in pure latine or doulce frenche, fewe men in consultations shulde (in myne opinion) compare with our lawyars, by this meanes beinge brought to be perfect orators, as in whome shulde than be founden the sharpe wittes of logitians, the graue sentences of philosophers, the elegancie of poetes, the memorie of ciuilians, the voice and gesture of them that can pronounce commedies, which is all that Tulli, in the person of the most eloquent man Marcus Antonius, coulde require to be in an oratour.[1]

Towards the end of the sixteenth century Kempe asked in his *Education of Children* that they should be taught not only to recognize 'euery trope, euery figure, aswell of words as of sentences; but also the Rhetoricall pronounciation and gesture fit for euery word, sentence, and affection'.[2] And Mulcaster, the famous headmaster of Merchant Taylors' School, makes the same demand, but at greater length, in *Positions*. His tenth chapter is devoted to the subject *Of lowd speaking, How necessarie, and how proper an exercise it is for a scholler*. And here he advocates 'the exercise of the voice which in Latin they name *vociferatio*'. Having described it, he notes that not only does it help an orator to sway his audience,

but for the help of learning, it is to some other verie good and great purpose, to pronounce without booke, with that kinde of action which the verie propertie of the subiect requireth, orations and other declamatory argumentes, either made by the pronouncer him selfe, or borrowed of some other.

Children who were too young to declaim even the simplest sentences should practise the exercise described by 'Antyllous, a verie olde Physician':

Those which were vnlearned said such things as they could remember, which were to be spoken aloud, and admitted any change of voice in

---

[1] Op. cit., p. 66.
[2] *The Education of Children* (1588), sig. G3r.

the vttering, now harshe and hard, now smoothe and sweete. Those
that were bookish recited either *Iambike* verses or *Elegies*, or other
such numbers, which with their currant carrie the memorie on, but
all without booke, as farre surmounting any kinde of reading. I haue
dwelt the longer in this exercise, bycause it is both the firste in rancke,
and the best meane to make good pronouncing of any thing, in any
auditorie, and therefore an exercise not impertinent to scholers.[1]

An even more detailed account of the methods of teaching
pronuntiatio to school-children is given by John Brinsley in
Ludus Literarius: Or The Grammar School. His advice is that

from the first entrance they be taught to pronounce euery thing
audibly, leasurely, distinctly, & naturally; sounding out specially the
last syllable, that each word may be fully vnderstood. But of this wee
haue spoken somewhat: & shall speake more in the due place, what a
grace sweete pronunciation giues vnto all learning, and how the want
of it doth altogether mar, or much deforme, the most excellent
speech.[2]

The boys should memorize Reusner's *Themes*, 'to help to furnish
them with variety of the best matter, and fit phrase. Besides
that, this will be a great furtherance to audacitie, memory,
gesture, pronuntiation.'[3]

Brinsley's book is written in the manner of a dialogue in
which one, Spoudeus, recounts his difficulties to the more experienced Philoponus, who replies with advice. This Spoudeus
has found 'passing hard to acquaint my schollars withall, to bring
them to any ripenesse or commendable faculty, but still they will
speake as a boy who is saying his lesson; though I haue both
directed them how to pronounce, vttering the sentences oft
before them, and haue very much called vpon them for the same'.
Philoponus, however, is prompt with a remedy:

To bring your schollars vnto this sweetnesse of pronuntiation, this
is the plainest and surest way, so farre forth as yet I can find; and
this I am assured will effect it in a commendable sort;

  1. You must remember that which was generally premised in the
beginning. To acquaint your young schollar from the very first

[1] *Positions* (1581), pp. 55–8.
[2] *Ludus Literarius* (1612), pp. 50–1.
[3] Ibid., p. 178.

entrance, to pronounce euery lesson and each word, audibly, leasurely, and distinctly, euer sounding out the last letter.

2. To pronounce euery matter according to the nature of it, so much as you can; chiefly where persons or other things are fained to speake.

As for example: In the *Confabulatiunculae pueriles*, Cause them to vtter euery dialogue liuely, as if they themselues were the persons which did speake in that dialogue, & so in euery other speech, to imagine themselues to haue occasion to vtter the very same things.

3. What they cannot vtter well in Latine, cause them first to do it naturally and liuely in English, and shew them your selfe the absurd-nesse of their pronuntiation, by pronouncing foolishly or childishly, as they do: and then pronounce it rightly, and naturally before them likewise, that they may perceiue the difference to be ashamed of the one, and take a delight in the other.

So cause them to do it after you, vntill they can do it in good sort, tuning their voices sweetly. When they can doe it in English, then cause them to doe it iust in the same manner in Latine.[1]

While it is probable that in this place Brinsley did not include gesture in his use of the term *Pronunciation*, it is obvious that he wanted the dialogues to be declaimed as if they were part of a play. The same method was to be used for Corderius, Esop's *Fables* and the plays of Terence. With Virgil's *Eclogues*, the boys were to be directed, 'yet still more liuely, in saying without booke to expresse the affections and persons of sheepe-heards; or whose speach soeuer else, which they are to imitate. Of which sort are the Prosopopeyes of Iupiter, Apollo, and others in Ouids Metamorphosis, Iuno, Neptune, AEolus, AEneas, Venus, Dido &c. Virgils AEneids.' And a note in the margin at this point observes: 'In all Authors wherein persons are fained to speak be carefull for this.'

Philoponus ends his advice on this subject as follows:

6. To help hereunto yet more, and that they may do euery thing according to the very nature; acquaint them to pronounce some speciall examples, set down in Talæus Rhetoricke as pathetically as they can: as examples of Ironies, Exclamations, Reuocations, Proso-popeyes, and those which are in his rules of pronouncing.

[1] Ibid., pp. 212–14.

Let them also be taught carefully, in what word the Emphasis lyeth, and therefore which is to be eleuated in the pronuntition. As namely those words in which the chiefe Trope or Figure is.

Thus let them take speciall pains to pronounce Theams or Declamations, striuing who shall doe best: and in all their oppositions to dispute, as if *ex animo* in good earnest, with all contention and vehemencie.

Finally, the practice of pronouncing emphatically, of some of Tullies Orations, which are most flowing in Figures of sentences (especially in Exclamations, Prosopopeis, Apostrophees, and the like: as some against Catiline) must needes much acquaint them with great variety of pronuntition, to be fitted for all sorts.

For more exquisite knowledge and practice hereof, I leaue it to the Vniuersities, which are to perfect all those faculties which are but begun in the Grammar Schooles; and do referre you to precepts to the seconde books of Talæus Rhetoricke *de pronunciatione*: or rather of Master Butlers Rhetoricke, as I said before.[1]

It is true that the final polish was given at the universities, or at the inns of court: nevertheless, instruction in pronouncing at school was not limited to such exercises as Brinsley outlines. The Elizabethan schoolboy took part in plays with the avowed object of practising his voice and gesture, of gaining confidence and poise for disputation and all other forms of public speaking. One of Richard Mulcaster's pupils, Sir James Whitelock, records that he and his fellows at Merchant Taylors' School acted in plays as part of their training in rhetorical delivery. 'And yeerly he presented sum playes to the court, in which his scholars wear only actors, and I on among them, and by that means taught them good behauiour and audacitie.'[2] In his *History of St. John's College, Cambridge*, Thomas Baker prints the ordinances made by Thomas Ashton, first headmaster of Shrewsbury School, under whom Sir Philip Sidney and his friend Fulke Greville were educated. According to the twenty-first ordinance:

Euerie thursdaie the Schollers of the first forme before they goo to

---

[1] Ibid.
[2] *The Liber Familicus of Sir James Whitelocke*, ed. Bruce (1858), p. 12.

plaie, shall for exercise declame and plaie one acte of a comedie, and euery Satterdaie versifie, and against mondaie morning ensuinge geue vpp their themes or epistles, and all other exercises of writinge or speakinge shalbe vsed in latten.[1]

Plays were performed for the same reasons at Winchester during the rule of Christopher Johnson in the sixties of the sixteenth century. Details concerning a Christmas play are given in a 'dictate'—written in Latin—which has survived in a notebook, belonging originally to William Badger, a pupil at Winchester from 1561 to 1569:

From those stage plays which we have lately exhibited publicly to the view I think you have derived this benefit besides others, that what must be pronounced with what expression, with what gestures not only you yourselves learned, but are also able to teach others, (if need were). For there should be in the voice a certain amount of elevation, depression and modulation, in the body decorous movement without prancing around, sometimes more quiet, at others more vehement, with the supplosion of the feet accommodated to the subject. These I remember I taught, all of which you expressed dexterously enough. It remains that you so remember that if anything hereafter be undertaken in a similar matter neither I shall seem to have lost my labour nor you the fruit of labour.[2]

At the universities, too, plays were performed for practice in rhetorical delivery. When John Rainolds of Corpus objected on moral grounds, William Gager, the Christ Church dramatist, replied (31 July 1592):

We contrarywise doe it to recreate owre selves, owre House, and the better parte of the Vniuersitye, with some learned Poëme or other; to practyse owre owne style eyther in prose or verse; to be well acquaynted with Seneca or Plautus; honestly to embowlden owre yuthe; to trye their voyces, and confirme their memoryes; to frame their speeche; to conforme them to convenient action; to trye what mettell is in evrye one, and of what disposition they are.[3]

---

[1] Ed. Mayor (1869), i. 411.
[2] Vide Baldwin, op. cit., i. 328.
[3] Corpus Christi College MS. 352, p. 48. See also F. S. Boas, University Drama in the Tudor Age, pp. 235-6.

In the *Apology for Actors*, Thomas Heywood buttresses his defence of 'lively and well spirited action' with the reminder:

Do not the Vniuersities, the fountaines and well-springs of all good Arts, Learning and Documents, admit the like in their Colledges? and they (I assure my selfe) are not ignorant of their true vse. In the time of my residence in *Cambridge*, I haue seen Tragedyes, Comedyes, Historyes, Pastorals and Shewes, publicly acted, in which Graduates of good place and reputation, haue bene specially parted: this is held necessary for the emboldening of their *Iunior* schollers, to arme them with audacity, against they come to bee imployed in any publicke exercise, as in the reading of Dialectike, Rhetoricke, Ethicke, Mathematicke, the Physicke, or Metaphysicke Lectures. It teacheth audacity to the bashfull Grammarian, beeing newly admitted into the priuate Colledge, and after matriculated and entred as a member of the Vniuersity, and makes him a bold Sophister, to argue *pro et contra*, to compose his Sillogismes, Cathegoricke, or Hypotheticke (simple or compound) to reason and frame a sufficient argument to proue his questions, or to defend any *axioma*, to distinguish of any Dilemma, & be able to moderate in any Argumentation whatsoeuer.

To come to Rhetoricke it not onely emboldens a scholler to speake, but instructs him to speake well, and with iudgement to obserue his comma's, colons, & full poynts, his parentheses, his breathing spaces, and distinctions, to keep a decorum in his countenance, neither to frowne when he should smile, nor to make vnseemely and disguised faces in the deliuery of his words, not to stare with his eies, draw awry his mouth, confound his voice in the hollow of his throat, or teare his words hastily betwixt his teeth, neither to buffet his deske like a madman, nor stand in his place like a liuelesse Image, demurely plodding, & without any smooth & formal motion. It instructs him to fit his phrases to his action, and his action to his phrase, and his pronuntiation to them both.[1]

Elizabethan education, with its emphasis on rhetorical delivery, taught a large number of boys and men from an early age to associate public speaking, and the reading of the poets, with a discipline of voice and gesture: however incompetent individuals may have been, all who had received this schooling understood the relationship between acting and literature which alone made possible the triumphs of the Elizabethan dramatists:

[1] *An Apology for Actors* (1612), sigs. C3^v–C4^r.

moreover, the training given at school produced a reservoir of recruits—of varying degrees of competence, no doubt—for the theatrical companies. We have, in addition, to thank the school-masters and university teachers for creating an intelligent audience with enthusiasm and with the critical standards which mean so much to the development of a popular art. The Eliza-bethans met pronunciation in other places, as well as in the class-room or lecture-hall. Rhetorical delivery was practised by lawyers and statesmen, by public orators at official entries, and by the participators in triumphs, pageants, and public shows. It was very much the concern, too, of the preacher, whether Anglican or Separatist; and the Jesuits were the universally acknowledged masters in this art. In the opinion of Thomas Wright: 'If there were an excellent preacher, who were admirable not only for doctrine, but also for action, hee would serue as a glasse for euery oratour to behold the beauty or blots of his action.'[1] John Donne seems to have gained much of his reputation as a preacher from the trained 'comeliness' of his pronouncing; his use of art to express sincere fervour went far towards the con-quest of his audiences. This estimate of Donne is confirmed by an *Elegiack Knell*, the work of Jasper Mayne, of Christ Church.

> Yet have I seen thee in the Pulpit stand,
> Where one might take notes from thy look & hand
> And from thy speaking action bear away
> More Sermon then some Teachers use to say.
> Such was thy carriage, and thy gesture such,
> As could divide the heart, and conscience touch:
> Thy motion did confute, and one might see
> An error vanquish'd by delivery.[2]

It is true that there are no renaissance works which set out specifically to expound the theory and practice of stage-playing; nevertheless, once we know that the Elizabethans believed that actors and orators agreed for the most part 'in the substance of externall action', it becomes clear that a study of rhetorical

[1] Op. cit., pp. 179–80.
[2] J. Bulwer, *Chironomia* (1644), p. 20.

delivery can lead to an understanding of what was done on the stage. It is not enough to search for gestures used by orators which could also have been used by actors. In order to make the best use of our sources, we must examine the part played by comeliness of action, not merely in the theatre, but in the civilization of the renaissance as a whole; why it was that in a defence of stage-players, Heywood could turn to the teachings of the rhetoricians on the importance of delivery to an educated man:

for be his inuention neuer so fluent and exquisite, his disposition neuer so composed and formall, his eloquence and elaborate phrases neuer so materiall and pithy, his memory neuer so firme & retentiue, his pronuntiation neuer so musicall and plausiue, yet without a comely and elegant gesture, a gratious and bewitching kinde of action, a naturall and familiar motion of the head, the hand, the body, and a moderate and fit countenance, sutable to all the rest, I hold all the rest as nothing. A deliuery & sweet action is the glosse and beauty of any discourse that belongs to a scholler.[1]

I intend, therefore, to explain all that was envisaged by an Elizabethan when he referred to 'whatsoever is commendable to the grave orator'. This involves an account of the training required for *actio*, with details of how the voice and body were to be used. It will be possible, in addition, to explain the ability of the Elizabethan actors to declaim verse satisfactorily in the theatre with an increase rather than a loss of dramatic intensity and characterization. For a satisfactory account of decorum and character we need to consult renaissance works on psychology, moral philosophy, painting, and theology as well as the critics and grammarians to supplement and fill out the bare details given by the treatises on *actio* proper. In the most unlikely places, we may find a revealing account of a gesture, often symbolic, which, applied to the text of a play, brings a scene to life with the breath of Elizabethan performance.

At this point it is necessary to deliver a warning: I am not arguing for one moment that we should attempt to re-introduce

[1] Op. cit., sig. C4^r.

rhetorical delivery into our civilization, either in our schools or in our theatres. In this book I am concerned with giving an accurate account of what happened during the renaissance, and not with making the plea that it should happen again. Where I justify a practice, or a theory, which has fallen into disfavour to-day, I do so only in so far as I believe that justification from the renaissance point of view is essential if we are to understand Elizabethan culture. Indeed, if this book has any value at all, it lies essentially in the fact that a knowledge of Elizabethan acting explains, without necessarily justifying, the practice of the dramatists. In the light of this acting, and of the traditions on which it was based, we come to know the nature and the strength of the bond joining together the poet, his players, and their audience; and the Elizabethan theatre is seen, as indeed it was, as a place where fusion of voice, gesture, and imagination communicated to an audience the close mingling of emotion and intellect which has its expression in the dramatic poetry of that age.

II

RHETORICAL DELIVERY IN THE SCHEME OF HUMANIST LEARNING

IN their teaching of rhetorical delivery humanists were inspired by clearly formulated convictions respecting the nature of man and his place in the universe. They adhered to the normal Christian view of man as unique among the inhabitants of the earth in virtue of his rational soul. Reason had made him the link between heaven and earth in the ordered chain of the universe. Reason, moreover, was the divine part, by means of which human beings knew God; it showed itself in erect stature, grace of movement, beauty of body, and—most important of all from the point of view of education—in speech. This commonplace is repeated continually in renaissance and medieval writings. By Lydgate we are told:

> Al erthli beestis be muet of nature,
> Sauf onli man, which haueth auauntage
> Bi a prerogatiff aboue ech creature
> To vttre his conceit onli be langage.
> The soule be grace repressith al outrage,
> Namli whan resoun hath the souereynte
> To bridle passiouns of sensualite.
>
> Kynde onto man hath youen elloquence,
> A thyng couenable in especiall
> Whan that it is conueied bi prudence,
> To talke of mateeris that be natural
> And secrees hid aboue celestial,—
>
> .   .   .   .
> .   .   .   .
>
> God of al this hath graunted knowlechyng
> Onli to man bi wisdam and resoun
> .   .   .   .

This the poweer & the precellence
Youe vnto man, which is resonable,
That bi langage and bi elloquence
A man is tauht in vertu to be stable.[1]

Every plan, if it is to be successful, must take into account the
nature of the material to which it is to be applied, as well as
the purpose which is ultimately to be served. Here, then, is the
material of renaissance education: man, in an ordered universe,
but fallen man in a fallen world; man subject to continual in-
surrection from his irrational parts within, and to constant siege
by Satan from without; and at any moment, the victim of the
unpredictable whim of Fortune, the fickle instrument of an
abiding Providence. As for the purpose of sixteenth-century
education, it was still as in Lydgate's day, to teach men 'in vertu
to be stable'. The aim was to produce a human being who was
neither 'passion's slave', nor 'a pipe for Fortune's finger'. The
ideal was one whose reason guided him to withstand temptation,
to hold self in control, to turn from evil, and to know God, appre-
hending the divine will, even when it could not be recognized,
in the seeming eccentricity of Fortune's 'buffets and rewards'.
Milton, as so often, spoke for all Christians when he declared:
'The end then of learning is to repair the ruins of our first
parents by regaining to know God aright, and out of that knowledge to love him, imitate him, to be like him, as we may the
nearest by possessing our souls of true virtue, which being united
to the heavenly grace of faith makes up the highest perfection.'[2]

Humanist methods took advantage of the intimate connexion
between reason and speech to establish training in thought and
expression firmly and prominently in the curriculum, both at
school and university. Wilson is representative of the educational
thought of his age, when he tells us: 'Man (in whom is powred
the breath of life) was made at the first being an euerliuing
creature, vnto the likeness of God, endued with reason, and
appointed Lorde ouer all other thinges liuing.' The Preface to

[1] Op. cit., pp. 765–6.
[2] *Of Education*, ed. Wallace, *Milton's Prose* (1947), p. 146.

The Art of Rhetorique continues with an account of the descent into brutishness after the Fall, from which humanity was extricated by 'appointed Ministers' possessing 'the gift of vtteraunce, that they might with ease win folke at their will, and frame them by reason to all good order'. And it is in line with normal renaissance thought, that we are told:

And among all other, I thinke him most worthie fame, and amongst all men to bee taken for halfe a GOD: that therein doth chiefly and aboue all other excell men, wherein men doe excell beastes. For he that is among the reasonable of al most reasonable, and among the wittie, of al most wittie, and among the eloquent, of al most eloquent: him thinke I among all men, not onely to be taken for a singuler man, but rather to be coumpted for halfe a God. For, in seeking the excellencie hereof, the soner he draweth to perfection, the nyer he commeth to God, who is the cheefe wisedome, and therfore called God, because he is most wise, or rather wisedom it self.[1]

If Wilson seems extravagant in his admiration of an eloquent man, we would do well to consider how high were his standards, and how few men there have been in the whole history of the world, whom he would admit worthy of his enthusiasm.

So far as method is concerned, much was learnt from the example of the ancients; and in the matter of doctrine, all that was admirable in the pagan civilizations was taken into the service of a greater morality. To some modern eyes, the chief fault of these methods of education lies in the over-emphasis given to the techniques of literature and oratory. But their prominence can be justified, and indeed is demanded by so sound an appreciation of the task, its nature and object, as we are given by Erasmus. 'All knowledge falls into one of two divisions: the knowledge of "truths" and the knowledge of "words": and if the former is first in importance the latter is acquired first in order of time.'[2] The subject which taught this essential knowledge of 'words' was known throughout the renaissance as 'rhetoric'.

[1] Op. cit., sig. A7ᵛ.
[2] *De Ratione Studii* (1511), trans. Woodward, *Desiderius Erasmus concerning the Aim and Method of Education* (1904), p. 162.

The term, 'rhetoric', has a number of meanings to-day. It is often used simply of oratory, of the art of persuasion, a justifiable appeal to reason and emotion. But we also speak of 'rhetoric' as though it meant a spurious kind of logic, a mingling of pure and false reasoning, and a not wholly legitimate play on the emotions. Used thus, the word denotes a feigning of conviction and reasonableness, merely as a means of winning a case. And the term is also employed to-day to describe an ornate use of words, both in verse and prose, an 'exornation' which suggests that less care has been devoted to the matter than to the manner of expression. When considering the function of rhetoric in Elizabethan schooling it is best to ignore the modern meanings just mentioned. It would, of course, be folly to suggest that they are entirely absent from Elizabethan usage; Bacon, for instance, inveighs against the perversion of an art of expression into one of winning arguments at all costs. Nevertheless, when Elizabethans spoke of rhetoric in relation to schooling, they normally referred to a subject whose nearest modern equivalent is composition.

When taught as rhetoric, however, composition treated verse as well as prose, letters as well as orations, the writing and appreciation of epic and pastoral, of tragedy and comedy, as well as the formal themes and orations and the elementary exercises of the schoolroom. The thorough and comprehensive treatment of so many aspects of the subject in Elizabethan education ought not to be regarded as evidence of a confusion between literary and oral composition, nor between rhetoric and poetic. Whether it be in speaking or in writing, in verse or in prose, composition is always a matter of shaping ideas, of clothing them in words for expression. And training makes for efficiency. The process, of course, is not entirely the same in verse as in prose; but in so far as composition is involved, the two fall very much within the province of the rhetoric taught in renaissance England. The function of rhetoric can be more clearly appreciated if we consider it in relation to Grammar, the first part of the Trivium. Accidence and syntax treat the in-

flexion and ordering of words in individual languages, and in doing
so also distinguish one language from another. But composition
is involved, whatever language is used for expression; so that
the rules taught as rhetoric apply equally well to all. The liken-
ing of a woman to a rose is to call attention to qualities shared by
both, and to view each in the light of the other; and the simile
remains simile whether it is expressed in French or English, in
Latin, Greek, or Hebrew. If we make use of Latin we must
follow the syntax and accidence of Latin grammar; and if our
Latin simile is in verse, then the rules of prosody must be con-
sulted. But in each case the act of composition can legitimately
be considered the business of rhetoric.

It was orthodox renaissance practice to consider expression in
language as consisting of five processes. Each of these was given
separate treatment in rhetoric, under the following headings
respectively: invention, disposition, elocution, memory, and
pronunciation. Sir Thomas Wilson defines invention as 'the
finding out of apt matter, . . . a searching out of things true, or
things likely, the which may reasonablie set forth a matter, and
make it appeare probable'.[1] He is here considering invention
from the point of view of persuasion, whether in writing or
speaking. But this process is involved in every instance of composition, literary and oral, when the writer or speaker considers
what ideas belong to his subject, and may profitably be used in
his expression of it, whilst at the same time he decides from
what aspect or aspects he will treat them. Invention is involved
as much in the creation of an epic or a tragedy, as in the composition of a formal letter to the income-tax authorities. Disposition, Wilson's second 'point', is described in *The Art of
Rhetorique* as 'the setling and ordering of things inuented . . . an
apt bestowing, and orderly placing of things, declaring where
euery argument shall be set, and in what manner euery reason
shalbe applied for confirmation of the purpose'.[1] This, again, is
handling rhetoric more strictly from the point of view of oratory
and disputation; nevertheless, here, too, the process is one which

[1] Op. cit., p. 6.

takes place whenever ideas are expressed in language; even in the so-called 'stream of consciousness' school of writing a decision has to be taken as to the final order in which ideas are recorded for transmission; and in the more logically coherent forms of composition the author's thoughts, in the widest meaning of the word, have to be arranged or disposed in such a manner that each development of the theme is presented at the right moment, and in the position most suitable in relation to the whole. The founders of humanist education did not err when they prescribed analysis of the traditional forms of epic structure as part of the teaching of disposition at school.

According to some renaissance theorists, invention and disposition are the concern of logic, and should not be taught as part of rhetoric at all. Obviously a good case can be made in favour of leaving them to the teacher of logic; they are inevitably very much his concern. But whether they were to be handled by him, or by the teacher of rhetoric, invention and disposition must, in practice, still exercise the pupils in a discipline which exerts a strong effect on literature and oratory. Wilson was apparently well aware that in these matters logic and rhetoric overlap: and although he treated invention as part of the latter, he noted: 'The places of *Logique*, giue good occasion to finde out plentifull matter. And therefore, they that will proue any cause, and seeke onely to teach thereby the trueth, must search out the places of *Logique*, and no doubt they shall finde much plentie.'[1] The difference between the two schools of thought was one of emphasis, rather than of principle; each agreed that invention and disposition must be taught; the difference concerned only the circumstances and the manner of teaching. As for elocution, memory, and pronunciation, they, by common consent, were taught as rhetoric.

While the word 'elocution' was already acquiring its modern meaning in the seventeenth century, its primary sense, to Dryden as to Bacon, was style, the adequate expression of thought and emotion in language perfectly suited to the subject

[1] Ibid.

as that exists in the author's mind. It was to gain this faculty of expression that the renaissance school-child was made to memorize the tropes and figures and to learn their appropriate uses. As a result, whilst elocution demanded the mechanical learning of schemes and tropes, and their functions, it also included practice in composition, together with close study of those works of the past which exemplified theory most effectively. Pupils were taught to deal with their own problems by careful examination of what had been done by classical authors in similar situations before them. The guiding principle has been enunciated by Erasmus: 'For it is not by learning rules that we acquire the power of speaking a language, but by daily intercourse with those accustomed to express themselves with exactness and refinement, and by the copious reading of the best authors.'[1] The key to style, as to everything else, lies in practice: 'whatever the form, whether prose or verse, or whatever the theme, write, write, and again write'.[2]

In conjunction, the two statements help to explain the practice known as *imitatio*. The work of others could enable a pupil to distinguish between what was suitable and unsuitable to the subject on which he himself was engaged. Thus, success often meant close dependence at first on one or more models, but this did not necessarily lead to plagiarism in the long run. *Imitatio* was a method of working and an acquired habit of mind; the term can also be used of the training needed to acquire the habit and to learn the method. Ascham refers to these meanings when he discusses the second and third kinds of imitation. The second, he says:

is to folow for learning of tonges and sciences the best authors. Here riseth, emonges proude and enuious wittes, a great controuersie, whether one or many are to be folowed: and, if one, who is that one; *Seneca* or *Cicero*; *Salust* or *Cæsar*; and so forth in Greeke and Latin.

The third kinde of *Imitation* belongeth to the second: as, when you be determined whether ye will folow one or mo, to know perfitlie, and which way to folow, that one; in what place; by what meane and

[1] Op. cit., p. 164.　　　　　　[2] Ibid., p. 165.

order; by what tooles and instrumentes ye shall do it; by what skill and iudgement ye shall trewelie discerne whether ye folow rightlie or no.[1]

The object of teaching *imitatio* at school as part of elocution was to train the pupil to understand his models, so that the fact of their existence, and the reactions which they stimulate, once known, should be absorbed organically into his own mental life. In Erasmus's words: 'A literal reproduction of the matter taught is, of course, not required, but the substance of it presented in the pupil's own way.'[2] Vives agrees: 'Little by little you will mix your own composition until the time when your stage of erudition has developed, your writing can become all your own.'[3] Ascham gives an account of a scheme for teaching imitation, which was partly the work of Sir John Cheke:

But if a man would take his paine also, whan he hath layd two places of *Homer* and *Virgill* or of *Demosthenes* and *Tullie* togither, to teach plainlie withall, after this sort:

1. *Tullie* reteyneth thus moch of the matter, thies sentences, thies wordes:

2. This and that he leaueth out, which he doth wittelie to this end and purpose.

3. This he addeth here.

4. This he diminisheth there.

5. This he ordereth thus, with placing that here, not there.

6. This he altereth and changeth, either in propertie of wordes, in forme of sentence, in substance of the matter, or in one or other conuenient circumstance of the authors present purpose.

In thies fewe rude English wordes are wrapt vp all the necessarie tooles and instrumentes, where with trewe *Imitation* is rightlie wrought withall in any tonge.[4]

Teachers were also advised to direct each pupil towards the models most suitable to his individual disposition. According to Vives:

There must be exact observation as to the kind of oratory towards which the disposition of the youth is suited (for wise men consider

---

[1] *The Schoolmaster* (1570), ed. Gregory Smith, *Elizabethan Critical Essays* (1937), i. 7–8. [2] Op. cit., p. 177.
[3] *De Ratione Studii Puerilis* (1523), trans. Foster Watson, *Vives and the Renascence Education of Women* (1912), p. 245. [4] Op. cit., p. 9.

this is to be noted in all the instruction of life), in order that each may apply himself to that to which he is inclined by his natural impulse, provided only he is not disposed to step towards the vicious, but is attached to the virtuous. . . . The scholar may make an attempt on his own account, but in his earlier years he should write under the supervision of his teacher; later, as he has made further progress, by himself alone. But if his disposition should lead him into faults, e.g. copiousness of words, to the point of exuberant redundancy; or parsimony of words, to the extent of becoming arid and devoid of force, then the scholar should be led back into a right and sound course by imitation of a different style.[1]

To claim that the Elizabethans never plagiarized, neither at school nor later in life, would be to show rather too naïve a faith in human nature. Nevertheless, we should not allow incidental plagiarism to blind us to the successes achieved by imitation; the teachers of the renaissance were merely attempting to perfect and operate a drill, which would strengthen and direct towards its maximum efficiency what is after all a normal and spontaneous function of the mind. Anyone who has read or seen, and at the same time imagined, *King Lear* can hardly treat a conflict between parent and daughter without what has been experienced through Shakespeare's play contributing its share in composition, however far from the surface of consciousness the contribution might be made. And those of us who have not known royalty, often find, on analysis, that our conception of kingship owes much to what Shakespeare has suggested, whether through the person of Richard III, of King John, or of Henry V. To make use of what one's mental life has absorbed from literature and art in this way, is merely to practise in a desultory and often undisciplined manner what the Elizabethans were taught to do systematically as imitation. They tried not so much to impose a discipline, as to resolve a natural function of the mind into constant and efficient order. There are many to-day who will object, like Ascham's 'ignorant, vnlearned, and idle student, or some busie looker vpon this litle poore booke', that imitation is the enemy to creative originality. 'They will say

[1] *De Tradendis Disciplinis*, pp. 191–2.

it were a plaine slauerie, and iniurie to, to shakkle and tye a good witte, and hinder the course of a mans good nature, with such bondes of seruitude, in folowyng other.'[1] But despite all the objections which can be raised against imitation, we must recognize that it was taught, and we cannot undo the results of that teaching in so far as they are embodied in Elizabethan drama, in the plays of Shakespeare as in those of all his contemporaries. The success of the method was due no less to careful exposition of literature in class than to the memorizing of figures and exercises in practical composition. Erasmus gives us a detailed account of the manner in which the poets should be treated by schoolmasters.

In reading a classic let the Master avoid the practice, common to inferior teachers, of taking it as the text for universal and irrelevant commentary. Respect the writer, and let it be your rule to rest content with explaining and illustrating his meaning. This would be the method I advise, say, in taking a class through a play of Terence. You begin by offering an appreciation of the author, and state what is necessary concerning his life and surroundings, his talent, and the characteristics of his style. You next consider comedy as an example of a particular form of literature, and its interest for the student: the origin and meaning of the term itself, the varieties of Comedy and the Terentian prosody. Now you proceed to treat briefly and clearly the argument of the play, taking each situation in due course. Side by side with this you will handle the diction of the writer; noting any conspicuous elegance, or such peculiarities as archaism, novel usage, Graecisms; bringing out anything that is involved or obscure in the phrases or sentence-forms; marking, where necessary, deviations and orthography, metaphors and other rhetorical artifices. Parallel passages should next be brought under notice, similarities and contrasts in treatments observed, and direct borrowings traced—no difficult task when we are comparing a Latin poet with his Greek predecessors. The last factor in the lesson consists in the moral applications which it suggests; the story of Orestes and Pylades, or of Tantalus, are obvious examples.[2]

By such methods the pupils were taught to appreciate that the words used by an author should be a sensitive record of the

[1] Op. cit., p. 10.   [2] De Rat. Stud., ed. cit. pp. 173-4.

exact quality of the thought and emotion in his mind. How far the average schoolmaster lived up to Erasmus's ideal may be doubted; but ample evidence exists that his admonitions bore some fruit. Palsgrave's edition of *Acolastus* (1540), for instance, which was annotated for use in class, would enable a master to fulfil the demands of Erasmus quite easily.[1]

Elocution is one side of a medal, whose other reads 'pronunciation'. According to Bulwer, 'the Speech and Gesture are conceived together in the mind'. And, again, he refers to the intimacy of the connexion in *Cautio XXIV* of *Chironomia*. 'The gestures of the *Hand* must be prepar'd in the Mind, together with the inward speech, that precedes the outward expression.'[2] It appears from these statements that not only the sound, but also the gestures, could be imagined at the moment when thoughts were turned into language in the mind. I do not know how far we are justified in taking Bulwer's words on this count as evidence of the normal attitude of his contemporaries. It may well be that they would have assented as a matter of course if the question had been put to them. But this point is not among those commonplaces of rhetorical delivery which are treated in even the most perfunctory sketches of the subject; it is possible, then, that the idiosyncrasy which led Bulwer to prepare a most valuable treatment of 'manuall rhetoric' and to include plates of illustrations, may also have inspired him to bedeck his hobby-horse as Pegasus on this single occasion. Nevertheless, as we have seen already, pronunciation was normally regarded as a legitimate and essential use of voice and body to communicate as accurately as possible the exact flavour and quality of the speaker's or writer's thought and emotion. Invention makes choice of ideas, disposition arranges them, whilst elocution shapes and clothes them in words. As the ideas themselves determine the style, the choice and arrangement of words, so style in its turn controls delivery. Thus there is a clear channel, through style, from the ideas in the author's or speaker's head to their manifestation in minutely correspondent details of voice

[1] Ed. Carver (1937). [2] *Chirol.*, p. 4: *Chiron.*, p. 142.

and gesture. 'For though a man can finde out good matter and good wordes, though hee can handsomely set them together, and carie them very well awaie in his minde, yet it is to no purpose if he haue no vtterance, when he should speake his minde, and shewe men what he hath to saie. Vtterance therefore, is a framing of the voyce, countenaunce, and gesture after a comely maner.'[1] In the later seventeenth century, pronunciation began to suffer an eclipse in English schooling: nevertheless, as late as 1739, John Holmes included this couplet in his *Art of Rhetoric Made Easy*:

> Adorn with TROPES and FIGURES your *Oration*,
> By VOICE and ACTION grace *Pronunciation*.[2]

Of the five processes treated by rhetoric, one, memory, remains to be considered. It is obviously essential to all learning: 'the same is memorie to the mind, that life is to the bodie'.[3] And in the absence of a common-place book, memory is needed for imitation. But, as bad memory is a serious handicap to oratory in particular, the subject is given special emphasis by teachers of rhetoric. One of the fundamental principles laid down by Erasmus was that work in class must be based on memory. As we have seen in Chapter I, the curriculum of school after school demanded that lessons should be repeated 'without book', and with the correct use of voice and gesture. It is surely not necessary to stress the influence which this training must have exerted upon those who later became professional actors. And in addition to demanding mechanical learning by rote, the section of rhetoric known as memory enabled pupils to acquire a useful system of mnemonics. Wilson gives an interesting account of how to 'learne to haue places, and digest Images in them accordingly'. He tells us that some, as an aid to memory, will associate what they wish to remember with a picture or 'image'; this, in its turn, is associated with, or 'placed in', a feature of the face or body of the person in whose company the Elizabethan wishes to be reminded of the required information. 'As to make

---

[1] Sir T. Wilson, op. cit., p. 6.   [2] p. 75.
[3] Sir T. Wilson, op. cit., p. 209.

the nose, the eyes, the forhead, the haire, the eares, and other
partes to serue for places.' And we have Wilson's assurance that
'though it seeme straunge and foolish to them that knowe it
not, yet the learned haue taken this way, and doubt not but
maruailes may bee done, if one haue places readie made for the
purpose, and haue them fresh in his remembraunce.'[1] I believe
that a similar technique was used by Hamlet in his attempt to
ensure that the Ghost's commandment (I. v.) *R.103*

> all alone shall liue
> Within the Booke and Volume of my braine.

Wilson says that the 'places of memorie' are like wax or paper;
and the images 'like vnto Letters or a Seale'. An image placed is
'like wordes written'; and 'the vtteraunce and vsing of them, is
like vnto reading'. He insists that, 'as we doe reserue Paper, and
yet chaunge our writing, putting out wordes as occasion shall
serue, and setting others in their roume: so may we doe for the
Images inuented, chaunge our Picture oft, and reserue the
Papers'.[1] Hamlet first 'puts out' all 'trivial fond records' from
the paper in his 'book and volume'. He then chooses both as
Place and Image the false mouth of his uncle, Claudius. And
when the tables have made an even stronger record of the reality
beneath appearance, 'that one may smile, and smile and be a
villain', the image is firmly in its place—'So Vnckle, there you
are'. Now Hamlet can memorize his oath, so that it must inevitably be recalled by the mere fact of his uncle's presence.
The key-words by which the oath is recorded are the last which
the Ghost spoke on departing—'Adue, Adue, Remember me'.
Hamlet has performed two complementary operations each of
immense importance in Revenge Tragedy. Not only has he
imprinted on his memory, and on the consciousness of his
audience, the exact nature of a duty undertaken, but he has, a
moment earlier, performed symbolically an act of oblivion. I
would not go so far as to suggest that we are expected to assume
that he really forgets that he ever gave Ophelia 'ought' (III. i).
But the refusal to admit that gifts had been made is consistent

[1] Ibid., p. 213.

with his declaration that only the memory of his mother, his
father, and his uncle shall henceforth exist for him, so that nothing shall come between him and his vengeance. 'Get thee to a
nunnery', moreover, can be seen to be a not unnatural outcome
of having committeed to memory 'O most pernicious woman',
as all that the speaker is prepared to remember of his relations
with the sex.

Heroic Education is the name given to a work on this schooling,
of which rhetoric was so important a part. This tract, published
at London in 1657, from the pen of 'I. B. Gent', comes after the
great humanist period. But even here the author refers to
qualities, which, though they are not fundamental, and do not
'make a man commendable of themselves', are necessary to a
nobleman in so far as

they direct him towards vertue, and are joined to the divine graces of
his mind and spirit, especially in men of great quality, who will not
take any profession, and should only scorn to be altogether ignorant
of them. In this rank I place riding the great horse, fencing, musick
both of voice, and instruments, dancing, vaulting, plausibility of
speech, a graceful garb, and accort carriage, a handsome mind and
presence, and all other such like qualities which only concern his
behaviour, and comeliness of action, which indeed one should endeavour to have . . . but as ornaments, and embellishments, fitting
for men of rank and quality.[1]

Here, indeed, is the spirit in which Sidney wrote the *Arcadia* and
the *Apology for Poetry*. The professional actor needed 'plausibility of speech' and 'comeliness of action' to earn a living, as
Heywood, among others, tells us. But what was livelihood for
the low-born was merely an aspect of the noble spirit in his
superiors. They learnt pronunciation among all the other accomplishments necessary for the practice of virtue, thus making
manifest to the world that lustre which—in Peacham's words—
'Nobility, being inherent and Naturall, can have (as the Dia-

---

[1] *Heroic Education*, sigs. E5^r–E5^v. The adjective *accort* is not recorded
in the *Oxford English Dictionary*. It may be derived from the Italian *accorto*,
meaning 'alert'.

mond) . . . but onely from it selfe.'[1] Plausibility of speech and a suitable carriage are elements of that comeliness of action by means of which man, when his intellect is not clouded by brutishness, can show the image of his Maker. 'In Action, how like an Angel!' says Hamlet in the First Folio text of this ironic rendering of a typical panegyric on man as a rational being. There is no need to dwell any longer on the aims and ideals of Elizabethan education: let the reverent enthusiasm of Peacham's father, Henry Peacham the Elder, proclaim the glory of the civilization out of which the Elizabethan dramatist created his plays, and for which his actor performed them:

The principal instruments of mans help in this wonderfull effect, are those figures and formes of speech conteined in this booke, which are the frutefull branches of eloquution, and the mightie streames of eloquence: whose vtilitie, power, and vertue, I cannot sufficiently commend, but speaking by similitude, I say they are as stars to giue light, as cordials to comfort, as harmony to delight, as pitiful spectacles to moue sorrowfull passions, and as orient colours to beautifie reason.[2]

[1] *The Compleat Gentleman*, ed. Gordon (1906), p. 3.
[2] *The Garden of Eloquence* (1593), sigs. AB iii^v–AB iv^r.

III
ALL THE PARTS OF AN EXCELLENT ORATOR

IF we are to understand exactly what Flecknoe meant when he declared that Burbage and the ideal actor had 'all the parts of an excellent orator', we need to turn to the detailed accounts of the use of voice and gesture given in renaissance works on delivery. Most authorities treated the subject along the lines laid down by Quintilian: 'Cum sit autem omnis actio, ut dixi, in duas divisa partes, vocem gestumque, quorum alter oculos, altera aures movet, per quos duos sensus omnis ad animum penetrat adfectus.'[1] This division is maintained by Talaeus and, following him, by Fraunce: '*Vtterance* is a fit deliuering of the speach alreadie beautified. It hath two parts, *Voyce* and *Gesture*, the one pertaining to the eare, the other belonging to the eye.'[2] And the same point is made by Butler in his *Rhetoricae Libri Duo*, which became a standard text-book for the grammar schools in the first half of the seventeenth century. Apart from Talaeus, whose *Rhetorica* ran through many editions and was the subject of various commentaries, source books for elementary treatment were provided by Alstedius with his *Rhetorica* (1616), and Cresollius, the author of a number of works of which *Vacationes Autumnales: siue de perfecta oratoris actione et pronuntiatione* (1620) is most useful to modern readers. Bulwer, who often draws upon it, could, however, have found numerous other authorities to support his assertion that '*Action* accommodated to perswade by an apt enumeration of utterance, called by the Rhetoricians, *Pronunciation*,' is 'divided into the figure of the voice, and motion of the body'.[3]

Delivery is sometimes spoken of as being divided into three parts—the *vox*, *vultus*, *vita* to which Wright among others refers. But, even those writers who make the threefold division into

[1] Ed. cit., iv. 248–50.   [2] Op. cit., sig. H6ᵛ.
[3] *Chiron.*, p. 132.

voice, countenance, and life or motion, treat voice by itself first, and regard the other two as subdivisions of a second main section. I shall therefore follow the normal method, treating voice first.

We cannot reconstruct the Elizabethan declaiming voice with anything like accuracy. Nevertheless, it is possible to say to what uses the voice was put, both in the expression of emotion, and in the delivery of lines in such a way that their quality as literature could be experienced by listeners. These uses of the voice will be treated fully in Chapter IV; here I shall deal only with evidence which suggests that the voice of the Elizabethan orator and actor was quite unlike that used for Shakespeare on the modern English stage, and differed considerably, moreover, from the normal Elizabethan way of speaking informally in conversation. Vives mentions the declamatory voice in his *On the Causes of the Corruption of the Arts* (1531): 'if its nature is being investigated, it is the task of the philosopher; if the method of training it, of the singing teacher.'[1] And a study of the methods used in training helps to make clear the certainty of a great difference between the voice of the Elizabethan player and that of the actor on the modern stage. I have already quoted extracts from Mulcaster's account of the exercise *vociferatio* prescribed by Antyllous, to which reference was often made throughout the renaissance. The exercise was employed not only for training the voice in declamation, but for reasons of health, for dispersing the humours afflicting the chest and head. Thomas Newton's translation of Lemnius advises: 'And if thereto bee vsed a cleare and lowde reading of bigge tuned soundes by stops and certayne Pauses, as our comicall felowes now do, that measure rhetoricke by their peuish Rhythmes, it wil bring exceding much good to the breast and Muscles.'[2] So Thomas Hobbes sang aloud when he was in bed, '(not that he had a very good voice) but for his health's sake.'[3]

The renaissance as a whole paid much attention to what

---

[1] Vives, *De Causis Corruptarum Artium* (1531), ed. Majansius (1782), tr. R. Stein, *On the Causes of the Corruptions of the Arts*, Bk. IV, Chapter ii.

[2] *The Touchstone of Complexions* (1581), ff. 53^r–53^v.

[3] Aubrey, *Brief Lives*, ed. Clark (1898), i. 352.

Quintilian has to say on the training of the voice. His influence can be traced on Wilson: 'They that haue no good voyces by nature, or cannot well vtter their wordes, must seeke for helpe els where. Exercise of the bodie, fasting, moderation in meate and drinke, gaping wide, or singing plaine Song, and counterfeyting those that doe speake distinctly, helpe much to haue a good deliueraunce.'[1] Fraunce has similar directions:

The practise and exercise is all in all: learne therfore some such speach wherein are contained all, or most varieties of voyce, and oftentimes vse to pronounce the same in such order and with as great heed as if thou were to vtter it in some great assemblie. Walking a litle after supper, annoynting, moderation of diet, and such like bodilie pleasures keep the voyce in temper.[2]

Wilson complains: 'Musicians in England haue vsed to put gagges in childrens mouthes, that they might pronounce distinctly, but now with the losse and lacke of Musick, the loue also is gone of bringing vp children to speake plainly.'[3] We know that he is not correct in his lament that music was neglected in Elizabeth's England; and it appears that he was probably also mistaken in the assertion that the practice of 'gagging', still known to modern choirmasters, had been allowed to lapse. This exercise plays an important part in Act IV, Scene iii of Zouche's *Sophister*, published in London only three years before the closing of the theatres in 1642. The 'persons of the drama' are abstractions, one of whom, Fallacy, has entrusted a letter to the care of another, Ignoratio. It is the task of Ignoratio to read the message to the lady to whom it is addressed. To this end he is rehearsed in his part by Ambiguity:

Ambiguity: I'le help thee. Now, how canst thou speak?
　　　　　　He pronounces some of Falacies *Letters*.
It must be lowder, she will not indure a chamber voyce, thou must yawne Like one that gapes for a Benefice: open like an Oyster, that she may gather the pearles of thy speech.
　　　　　　　　　　　He goes on pronouncing.

<hr>

[1] Op. cit., p. 219.　　　　　　[2] Op. cit., sig. I7ʳ.
[3] Op. cit., p. 219.

Oh that we had some Peble-stones, such as *Demosthenes* used; but hold, it may be this will serve; Spare my fingers *he gags him.* but while I tell a hundred. I warrant thee this will make thee like a chirping Sparrow.

As Ignoratio and Ambiguity are thus engaged, the one with his fingers in the other's mouth, they are attacked and beaten in their defenceless state.[1]

The difference between a 'chamber voice' and that used for 'pronouncing' in the first half of the seventeenth century is mentioned by James Arderne. His *Directions Concerning the Matter and Style of Sermons* (1671) were written after the revolution which took place in the middle of the century with respect to declamation off the stage. The educated gentleman was now adjured to avoid the intricacies of the earlier style in both voice and gesture. As a result Arderne advises: 'you need not learn from the Stage (as *Tully* did from *Roscius*) how to behave your self: it is enough, that you pronounce cleerly & man-like, with some significant small inflexion of the voice, as the matter requires; yet so that it never differ from the familiar and natural sound.'[2] But we have seen that the subjects of Elizabeth and her first two successors were actually told to take stage-players for models of oratory, as in the days of Cicero and Roscius. The change that took place in rhetorical delivery during the seventeenth century is illustrated by Steele's remark, in No. 66 of *The Tatler*, that the English clergy were, in 1709, 'the most learned Body of Men now in the World; and yet this Art of Speaking, with the proper Ornaments of Voice and Gesture, is wholly neglected among them'.[3]

In those works in which earlier generations expounded the 'ornaments' whose loss Steele regrets, we often find that gesture is considered of greater account than voice. Chapter XVIII of MS. Ashmole 768 begins: 'Now followeth gesture an accion of

[1] R. Zouche, *The Sophister* (1639), IV. iii, sig. G4ᵛ.
[2] J. Arderne, *Directions Concerning the Matter and Style of Sermons* (1671), p. 95.
[3] *The Tatler* (1712).

far greater force then the voice.'[1] This work is orthodox, agreeing with Fraunce, for instance, in its few preliminary notes on 'the whole bodie', and then proceeding to a more detailed treatment of 'the partes of the bodie. And first for the head.' This is not to be moved except with the trunk, and is to be 'disposed according to the bodie'. Casting the head down is 'a sign of humylitie and modestie':[1] here, again, Fraunce agrees.[2]

It is hardly possible to treat the head without referring to the face and features. After saying that 'To make often gesture with the head alone is forbidden', Fraunce adds, 'But the chiefest force of the head is in the countenance, and of the countenance, in the eyes, which expres liuelilie euen anie conceit or passion of the mind: as therfore the face & countenance must bee comelilie and orderlie composed, so the eyes verie diligentlie are to be regarded.'[3] And the manuscript on rhetoric declares that 'to bend the brow is not comelie in an orator', adding that as with the eyes, 'which are the tokens of the minde,' much care must be taken: these must 'shew forth so maney changes as there are mocions in the minde'.[4] Unfortunately Bulwer did not carry out his expressed intention of writing a treatise on the use of the head; but it is clear that teachers of *actio* were at pains to inculcate such directions as are to be found in *The Passions of the Mind* and in Butler's *Rhetoric*, this latter containing a chapter entitled *De gestu capitis, frontis, oculorum*.[5]

Christopher Johnson's remarks on the use of the feet have already been quoted; it will be remembered that he told his pupils to acquire 'decorous movement without prancing around, . . . with the supplosion of the feet accommodated to the subject. These I remember I taught, all of which you expressed dexterously enough'.[6] Striking the ground with the foot obviously lends force to a passionate statement; but there is a reference to another 'action', which is difficult to visualize gravely. 'To ffriske the thighes togeather is a signe of indignacion and stirreth vpp

---

[1] *MS. Ashmole 768*, p. 541.   [2] Op. cit., sig. I8[r].
[3] Op. cit., sig. KI[r].   [4] *MS. Ashmole 768*, p. 541.
[5] Bulwer, *Chirol.*, sig. A7[v] and Butler, *Rhetoricae Libri Duo* (1629), sig. P2[v].   [6] See *supra*, p. 14.

the hearer. And to stampe with the foote in great contentions is not vnseemelie.'[1] A stage direction agreeing with this extract from MS. Ashmole 768 is to be found in *The True Chronicle History of King Leir and His Three Daughters*. Ragan is thus described, as she reads the letter brought to her from Goneril: '*She reads the letter, frownes and stamps*', and whilst she does this, the Messenger remarks:

> See how her colour comes and goes agayne,
> Now red as scarlet, now as pale as ash:
> She [*sic*] how she knits her brow, and bytes her lips,
> And stamps, and makes a dumbe shew of disdayne,
> Mixt with reuenge, and violent extreames.[2]

Most renaissance authorities agree with Quintilian in emphasizing the importance of the arm, hand, and fingers in rhetorical delivery. What is probably the fullest treatment in existence on this aspect of the art has been given by John Bulwer in the two works to which reference has already been made. He asserts that

the moving and significant extention of the *Hand* is knowne to be so absolutely pertinent to speech, that we together with a speech expect the due motion of the *Hand* to explaine, direct, enforce, apply, apparrell, & to beautifie the words men utter, which would prove naked, unlesse the cloathing *Hands* doe neatly move to adorne and hide their nakednesse, with their comely and ministeriall parts of speech.[3]

This passage may possibly lend force to the asseveration made in *Hamlet* (i. ii.) by Claudius as to his regard for Polonius:

> What would'st thou beg *Laertes*,
> That shall not be my Offer, not thy Asking?
> The Head is not more Natiue to the Heart,
> The Hand more Instrumentall to the Mouth,
> Then is the Throne of Denmarke to thy Father.

---

[1] *MS. Ashmole 768*, p. 541.
[2] *The True Chronicle History of King Leir and His Three Daughters* (1605), ed. W. W. Greg and R. W. Bond (1907), sigs. E1ʳ–E1ᵛ.
[3] *Chiron.*, p. 16.

FIG. 2

According to the title-page, *Chirologia* has for its subject, 'the Speaking Motions, and Discoursing Gestures'. They speak for themselves, and in so far as they do so they are related to mime. The book is divided into two sections, the first of which names and describes sixty-four gestures. Forty-eight of these are illustrated (Figs. 2, 3). The second section is entitled *Dactylogia: or the Dialects of the Fingers*. Here we are given twenty-five gestures, by means of which the hand, 'the great Artificer and active Contriver of most corporall conceits, receiving good intelligence of the patheticall motions of the minde, proves a *Summarie* or *Index*, wherein the speaking habits thereof significantly appear, representing in their appearance the present posture of the phansie. And as we can translate a thought into discoursing signes; so the conceptions of our minde are seen to abound in severall *Dialects* while the *articulated Fingers* supply the office of a voyce.'[1] Twenty-four of these gestures are illustrated (Fig. 4): the eighth, which does not appear among the 'Chirograms', is described in the text as 'The forefinger kissed in the naturall greetings of the *Hand*.'[2]

Whereas *Chirologia* treats the expression of emotion, 'the patheticall motions of the minde', *Chironomia* deals mainly with the correct way to use hand, arm, and fingers to reinforce the effect of elocution and disposition. The division is not strictly maintained in practice, though the intention is evident, both in the arrangement of material and in pronouncements on the respective title-pages. *Chironomia* is declared to handle the artificial 'managing of the hand' in the manner by means of which 'naturall GESTURES' can be refined into 'the Regulated Accessories or faire-spoken Adjuncts of RHETORICALL Utterance'. This remark is amplified within the book. The movements of the hands

shew the mentall springs from whence they naturally arise; so invited by Art to the aid of Eloquence, they become the Accessories and faire spoken Adjuncts of speech. Hence the first Artificers of Manuall Rhetoricke, hit on the right veine of Oratorie, when conducted by a

---

[1] *Chirol.*, p. 157.   [2] Ibid., p. 167.

FIG. 3

learned curiosity of wit they tooke in hand that polite device, and elegant design of reducing the usuall gestures of Nature into strict rules of Art, preparing the undigested motions of Nature, and making them more formall, and fit for the intention of Rhetoricke, whose life and force they made much to consist in the just demeanour of the *Hand*, whose motions appeare as emphaticall to the eye, as speech doth to the eare.[1]

Chironomia is divided into three sections. The first contains fifty-nine gestures of the hand, with examples of their use taken from a variety of sources such as ancient history and literature, and commentaries on the scriptures and law. Twenty-four of these gestures are illustrated (Fig. 5). The second section describes twenty-six 'Canons of the Fingers'; and here again there are twenty-four illustrations (Fig. 6). In the third section we are given a number of 'Praevarications' and 'Cautionary Notions', as a warning against what Bulwer calls 'solecisms' in the use of the hand.

How far is Bulwer's work to be taken as authoritative with respect to the acting and oratory of sixteenth-century and early seventeenth-century England? It can be said at once that, in so far as it is possible to check his work by comparison with other authorities, especially those to whom he refers, we are justified in relying on the descriptions of the gestures given in his text: moreover, he offers a faithful record of what his numerous sources have to say. Bulwer's 'Canon XL' of the *Canons of Rhetoricians Touching the Artificiall managing of the Hand in Speaking* tells us: 'Both *Hands* extended out forward together, is an Action commodious for them who *submit, invoke, doubt, speak* to, *accuse*, or *call by name, implore*, or *attest*.'[2] This gesture is inscribed *Addubitabit*; it is among the illustrations ('X' in Fig. 5). Fraunce describes the circumstances in which this gesture might be used, in his Chapter XXXII, *Of Addubitation*:

The conference or debating followeth, and it is either in asking, or in answering. In asking be conteined deliberation, and occupation, or preuenting and meeting with an obiection. Deliberation is, when we

---

[1] *Chiron.*, pp. 16–17.   [2] *Ibid.*, p. 55.

FIG. 4

aske and enquire in consultation wise: then when wee haue thus for
a while helde the auditors in suspence, we determine of somewhat
eyther more or lesse contrarie to their expectation. Deliberation is
either in Addubitation, or communication. Addubitation or doubting
is a kinde of deliberation with our selues.[1]

In another part of the book he says, 'the left hand ioyned with
the right is fit for addubitations or doubts, & obtestations or
prayers, & verie much frequented'.[2] Whilst the two hands are
together in both doubts and prayers the difference between the
two gestures can be observed by comparing Bulwer's *Addubitabit* with his *Oro* (marked 'B' in Fig. 2). Fraunce's gesture for
'urging' is as follows: 'The former finger stretched out doth
point or showe, when the other three are closed and kept in with
the thumbe. . . . If it be turned directly downe towards the
ground, it vrgeth.'[3] Bulwer illustrates this gesture ('P' in Fig. 6).
He gives this description as *Canon* XXII: 'The *Index* (the rest
compos'd into a *Fist*) turn'd down perpendicular; doth *urge*,
inculcate and drive the point into the heads of the Auditours.'[4]

Bulwer insists that he is not repeating all the details of an
obsolete art of the Ancients; he says: 'we are not to tread in their
steps so far, as to revoke [i.e. *recall, call back*] the whole Art of
their obsolete Rhetorique.'[5] Nevertheless, he names as one of
his chief sources Quintilian, 'unto whose curious observation in
the *Hand*, I referre those who out of curiositie desire to be more
punctually informed in these most subtle and abstruce notions
of the *Hand*.'[6] He does not claim complete accuracy for his
pictures; but having felt the need, he had been moved to supply
'Types and Chirograms, whereby this Art might be better
illustrated then by words'.[7] He apologizes: 'If I have miscarried
in any, it is the more pardonable, since in all my search after
these subtleties of the *Hand*, I never met with any Rhetorician
or other, that had picturd out one of these Rhetoricall expressions of the Hands and fingers; or met with any Philologer that

[1] Op. cit., sig. G7^r.
[2] Ibid., sig. K3^r.
[3] Ibid., sigs. K3^v–K4^r.
[4] *Chiron.*, p. 79.
[5] Ibid., p. 131.
[6] Ibid., p. 25.
[7] Ibid., p. 26.

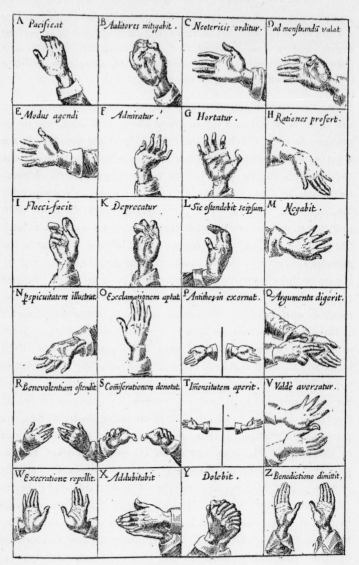

FIG. 5

could exactly satisfie me in the ancient Rhetoricall postures of *Quintilian*.'[1] He regretted, in addition, that 'the necessary defect of these Chirograms in point of motion and percussion, which Art cannot expresse, must be supplied with imagination, and a topicall reference to the order and number of their Gestures'.[2]

Despite his own disclaimer, however, one of Bulwer's 'chirograms' elucidates a passage written a hundred years earlier in Richard Sherry's *Treatise of Schemes and Tropes*. At one point Sherry apologizes because 'I haue not made the matter here so perfecte as my wyll and desyer is that it shoulde haue ben, and that I haue but briefelye touched, and as it were with my litle fynger poynted to these thinges, which require a lenger declaracion'.[3] To point with the little finger is illustrated by Bulwer with the title *Leviter tangit* (marked 'S' in Fig. 6). He describes the gesture as follows:

If the Ring *Finger* by a single Action goe out of the open *Hand*, as it were to serve the Tact, it may much advance their utterance, who in discourse touch and handle a matter lightly.

This is a Magistrall notion of my owne, never thought on by any Ancient or Moderne Rhetorician, for all I can finde, (unlesse *Quintilians Interim Quartus oblique reponitur*, darkely allude unto it) but, grounded upon the same principles of observation as all their precepts of gesture are. *Galen* saies this is the *Finger* we use to put out when we would touch any thing lightly; and the ancient Physitians used gently to stir their cordialls; and *Collyriums* with this *Finger*, thence called *Medicus*, upon which ground of Nature, I was induced to cast in my mite into the treasury of this Art.[4]

According to Ben Jonson the 'Ring Finger' is the third:[5] if this is placed in accordance with Bulwer's directions, the hand is held in a posture which could be described as pointing with the little finger; this is clearly to be seen in his illustration. Another piece of evidence to support Bulwer's description of what he claims to have observed is provided by Giovanni Bonifaccio's *L'Arte di Cenni*, published at Vicenza in 1616. Of 'Mostrar il dito

---

[1] *Chiron.*, p. 26. [2] *Chirol.*, p. 150.
[3] R. Sherry, *A Treatise of Schemes and Tropes* (1550), sig. A7ᵛ.
[4] *Chiron.*, p. 82.
[5] *The Alchemist* (i. iii), ed. Herford and Simpson, v. 310.

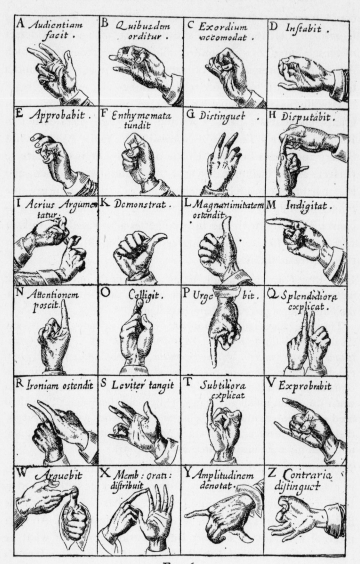

A *Audientiam facit .*	B *Quibusdem orditur .*	C *Exordium accomodat .*	D *Instabit .*
E *Approbabit .*	F *Enthymemata tundit*	G *Distinguet .*	H *Disputabit .*
I *Acrius Argumentatur .*	K *Demonstrat .*	L *Magnanimitatem ostendit .*	M *Indigitat .*
N *Attentionem poscit .*	O *Colligit .*	P *Urge bit .*	Q *Splendidiora explicat .*
R *Ironiam ostendit*	S *Leviter tangit*	T *Subtiliora explicat*	V *Exprobrabit*
W *Arguebit*	X *Memb : orati : distribuit*	Y *Amplitudinem denotat .*	Z *Contraria distinguet*

FIG. 6

minimo', he says: 'Il gesto di mostrar questo picciol dito accenna persona, o cosa minima, e di pochissima consideratione, e debolissima; come col mostrar il pollice habbiamo detto accennarsi fortezza, e robustezza. Vi è il prouerbio: Vno digitolo, che si dice di far alcuna cosa con pochissima fatica, e facilmente.'[1]

We still have to consider, however, the possibility that Bulwer's compilations represent a case of special pleading: that his enthusiasm for his chosen subject has led him to panegyrics which would not have been generally endorsed. But Fraunce, who is certainly not interested in special pleading, states boldly: 'Without the hand the gesture is nothing'.[2] And MS. Ashmole 768 tells us: 'The Arme must be in contynuall mocion either this waie, or that waie as the matter requireth.' And later: 'The apte composicion of the fingers is seemelie.'[3] As late as 1652, moreover, John Gaule, in his *The Mag-astro-mancer*, speaks of many things 'done by a prompt subtlety and industry of hand; of which sort we see some are done daily by Stageplayers and juglers, which therefore we call Chirosophists, that is, slight-handed'.[4] We are justified, then, in accepting at their face-value the eulogies with which Bulwer, the self-styled *Philochirosophist*, describes the effect of 'manual rhetoric' upon the society for whom Elizabethan drama was written:

upon a sudden, and the least signification of the mind, you may shew the glittering orbes of Heaven, and the gaping jawes of Earth. Sometimes place your arguments upon your *Fingers*; sometimes lifting up your *Hands*, threaten and denounce punishment, or with a rejecting posture, abominate: sometimes shake and brandish your Hand as the lance of Elocution; that so you may be ready for all varietie of speech, and attaine that ὀξυχειρίαν or facilitie of action, with the decorum & beauty of decent motion: which excells both that of colours and proportion.[5]

The emphasis placed on the use of *gestus* in the account of rhetorical delivery which I have taken from renaissance sources

---

[1] G. Bonifaccio, *L'Arte di Cenni* (1616), p. 341.
[2] Op. cit., sig. K3ʳ.   [3] *MS. Ashmole 768*, p. 541.
[4] J. Gaule, *The Mag-astro-mancer* (1652), sig. I 4ʳ.
[5] *Chiron.*, p. 141.

may be so heavy as to suggest that to follow the directions of the theorists would be to indulge in an art of tedious affectation, far removed in spirit from those energies of poetry and action which are among the outstanding qualities of Elizabethan drama. And, indeed, we may find that pedantry in gesture is as plentiful as pedantry in words. There is the French preacher, Oliver Maillard, whose sermon, preached in 1500, is marked 'hem, hem, hem', where he intended to cough: in other sermons of his, moreover, the directions 'clama' and 'percute pede' are found.[1] Works on preaching written during the eighteenth century and the early nineteenth century abound in warnings against affectation in delivery, often justifying themselves by recalling Addison's paper in No. 407 of *The Spectator*.[2] That Shakespeare's age was equally subject to affected *pronuntiatio* is apparent from warnings such as those by Bulwer, who distinguishes between the style suited to the French and Italians, and that befitting an Englishman, with whom moderation and gravity 'in gesture is esteemed the greater virtue.'[3] But the theorists in general emphasize the fact that they are merely recording what was done both in and before the renaissance, by the most talented speakers in the civilized world, and with marked success. Theory, here, has its origin in a careful observation of what worked in practice. And as for affectation, there is a constant stream of warnings against it in the very works which might seem affected to modern inhibitions. The writer of MS. Ashmole 768, immediately after his call for 'apte composicion' of the fingers, added, 'but conceipte in it is altogeather vncomelie'.[4] The very fulness with which Bulwer has treated his subject results in planting in the modern mind a suspicion that the art which he has described could not have been 'natural'. I shall therefore turn to him alone for evidence with which to rebut the charge which his wealth of detail is apt to encourage. But first it is necessary to be quite clear as to what can legitimately be meant

---

[1] F. P. Wilson, 'Table Talk' (*Huntington Library Quarterly*, 1940), IV. i. 31.
[2] Ed. G. Gregory Smith (1897), vi. 42–4.
[3] *Chiron.*, p. 145.
[4] p. 541.

by 'natural' or 'unnatural' in this context. An opera singer who sings badly can be, and often is, called 'unnatural' without any violence to logic and good sense. But, on the other hand, a man who sings perfectly, especially with *bel canto*, is by no means behaving 'naturally' in the sense that the acting of a modern drawing-room drama is 'natural'. In singing it is possible to be 'natural' without being naturalistic; the same is true of rhetorical delivery. Bulwer actually uses 'unnatural' to describe an action which is so completely natural as to have its awkwardness quite unredeemed by the refinement of art: this is a usage which would be normal to-day in a parallel case in opera or ballet. 'To use the *Middle-Finger* instead of the *Index* in points of demonstration' is, he tells us, 'an action so unnaturall and uncomely, that we will not permit children to be guilty of committing it.'[1] Whoever tries pointing in this way, with the 'fooles *Index*', and remembers to add a suitable expression of the face and posture of the body, will find himself performing an 'action' which illustrates admirably Hamlet's discontented avowal (II. ii.).

> Yet I,
> A dull and muddy-metled Rascall, peake
> Like Iohn a-dreames, vnpregnant of my cause,
> And can say nothing.

According to *Chironomia*, 'to use no Action at all in speaking, or a heavy and slow motion of the *Hand*, is the propertie of one stupid and sluggish'.[2] Nevertheless, the reverse in itself was not commended. 'Such who have Hands too active in discourse, and use to beat the aire with an odious kinde of *Chiromachia*, bewray the cholerique transportation of their individuall natures, a habit of the *Hand* incident to young men.'[3] He states firmly: 'Shun affectation: for all affectation is odious: and then others are most moved with our actions, when they perceive all things to flow, as it were, out of the liquid current of Nature.'[4] He is never tired of repeating this theme. 'Nature exhorts all men to

---

[1] *Chiron.*, pp. 120–1.   [2] Ibid., p. 115.
[3] Ibid., p. 111.   [4] Ibid., p. 138.

Action consentaneous to the stile of their Elocution. . . . Art
being the Imitator which perfects Nature.'[1] And again: 'the
ancient Rhetoricians, who cast their eyes upon Nature, and insisted in her steps, whose Art was principally bent to imitate the
severall actions of the Mind with a decent and comely grace;
admitted no gesture to the *hand*, but what they did find by an
accurate collation to have some similitude with the truth of
Nature'.[1] Bulwer was in complete agreement with this spirit.
Cautio III of the 'Cautionary Notions' in *Chironomia* sums up:

> There are two kinde of Actions, which are more perceived in the
> motion of the *Hand*, than any other part of the Body: one, that
> Nature by passion and ratiocination teacheth; the other, which is
> acquired by Art. An Oratour is to observe both the Naturall and the
> Artificiall; yet so, that he adde a certaine kinde of art to the Naturall
> motion, whereby the too much slownes, too much quicknes, and im-
> moderate vastnesse may be avoyded.[2]

Faced with this statement we see that Bulwer was fully
justified when he declared: 'In all Action, Nature beares the
greatest sway . . . a Rhetorician . . . must take counsell of Nature
for the framing of the complexionall and individuall properties
of his *Hand*.'[3] In a passage to which I have already referred,
Thomas Wright told orators to observe men in real life speaking
passionately, but to 'leaue the excesse and exorbitant leuitie or
other defects, and keepe the manner corrected with prudent
mediocritie'. And after telling us that this is done by the stage
players who 'act excellently', he added another observation, not
yet quoted: 'for as the perfection of their exercise consisteth in
imitation of others, so they that imitate best, act best'.[4] None-
theless it becomes clear from both his and Bulwer's insistence
upon correction of 'defects' and upon the doctrine that Art is
'the Imitator which perfects Nature', that naturalistic imitation
is not intended.

Although much emphasis is laid upon the need to use the
hands correctly we are also told: 'Both *Hands* doe sometimes

---

[1] *Chiron.*, pp. 20–1.   [2] Ibid., p. 132.
[3] Ibid., p. 143.   [4] Op. cit., p. 179.

rest, and are out of action: yet this Rhetoricall silence of the *Hand*, is an act proper, where no affection is emergent: though a long intermission of gesture be displeasing.'[1] When in motion the hand must travel from left to right. Bulwer's Cautio VI states: 'Gesture doth with most conformity to Art, begin at the left Hand, the sentence beginning together from the left side, but is put off and laid downe at the *Right Hand*, together with the end of the sentence.' And *Cautio VII:* ' 'Tis absurd often to change gesture in the same sentence, or often to conclude sinister motions.'[2] But the movements of the arm and hand, like those of the rest of the body, were accommodated in general to the voice and meaning. According to MS. Ashmole 768: 'Of the whole bodie the generall rule is, that the gesture be correspondent to the ordering of the voice.'[3] Fraunce observes: 'The gesture must followe the change and varietie of the voyce, answering thereunto in euerie respect.'[4] It was not merely an actor's thought, but that of any man schooled in the first principles of Elizabethan learning, which went into the passage (in the Quarto version), in which Titus Andronicus refused to speak without his right hand, asking (v. ii.),

> how can I grace my talke,
> Wanting a hand to giue that accord.[5]

The detailed treatment of this concurrence between meaning, voice, and gesture will be given in Chapter IV; nevertheless, it is necessary to emphasize at this point that every effort was made to avoid monotony. Fraunce's words above assume a 'change and varietie of the voyce'; and Bulwer's Cautio XV begins: 'Take care that variety of gesture, may answer the variety of the voice and words.'[6] Cautio XIV has just told us: 'Shun similitude of gesture; for as a monotone in the voyce, so a continued similitude of gesture, and a *Hand* always playing upon one string is absurd, it being better sometimes, to use a

---

[1] *Chiron.,* p. 143.   [2] Ibid., p. 133.
[3] *MS. Ashmole 768*, p. 541.
[4] Op. cit., sig. I7^v.
[5] Quarto (1594), sig. I3^r, and Quarto of 1600, sig. I2^v.
[6] *Chiron.*, p. 138.

licentious and unwarrantable motion, then alwayes to obtrude the same Coleworts.'[1]

The manner in which the body was accommodated to voice and meaning constituted one of the greatest differences between the acting of oratory and that of the stage. When Fraunce had directed that gesture should change with the voice he added: 'yet not parasiticallie as stage plaiers vse, but grauelie and decentlie as becommeth men of greater calling.'[2] The same warning comes from Bulwer for the hand. 'Gesture must attend upon every flexion of the voice, not Scenicall, but declaring the sentence and meaning of oure minde, not by demonstration, but signification: for it must be accommodated by the *Hand*, that it may agree and have a proper reference, not so much to the words, as to the sense.'[3] Another caution against miming says:

To represent a Physitian feeling the pulse of the arteries, which with them is *manum mittere in carpum*; or To shew a Lutenist striking the chords of an instrument, are kind of expressions to be avoided; for an Oratour should bee farre from any light imitation of a Dancer, and is not permitted to shew what hee speakes, but his gesture must more expresse his sense, then his words.[4]

This applied to the trunk, too. 'Let the bodie therefore with a manlike and graue motion of his sides rather followe the sentence than expresse euerie particular word. Stand vpright & straight as nature hath appoynted: much wauering and ouercurious and nice motion is verie ridiculous',[5] says Fraunce: and in another place: 'For the feete; it is vndecent to stand waggling now on one foote, now on another. To strike the ground with the foote was vsuall in vehemencie of speach. To stirre a step or two is tollerable, so that it be seldome.'[6] The Bodleian manuscript also insists, that, 'for the trunke of the bodie, an oratour must looke that it be moved after a sober and graue manner, and not as amongst the stage-players'.[7] The author of the manuscript agrees with Fraunce that 'to walke may be sometyme permitted

---

[1] *Chiron.*, p. 136.
[2] Op. cit., sig. I7^v.
[3] *Chiron.*, pp. 133–4.
[4] Ibid., p. 103.
[5] Op. cit., sig. I7^v.
[6] Ibid., sig. K4^v.
[7] Op. cit., p. 541.

to an Oratour, but verie seldome'.[1] Christopher Johnson at Winchester, it will be recalled, also permitted his scholars to supplode, but did not want them to 'prance' about the stage. Graceful movement like that of a dancer was so much a part of the professional actor's performance that Cornelius Agrippa described his 'Rhetorisme' as 'Rhetoricall daunsing, not vnlike that of the stage players', with the observation that it was still practised 'of some staged Fryers'. The injunction against too much use of the feet in oratory seems to have affected the style of academic players even in the full performance of a play. In *The Return from Parnassus: or The Scourge of Simony* (performed at Cambridge in 1601–2, Burbage points out that the university actors 'haue oftentimes a good conceite in a part'. Kemp replies:

Its true indeede, honest *Dick*, but the slaues are somewhat proud, and besides, tis a good sporte in a part, to see them neuer speake in their walke, but at the end of the stage, iust as though in walking with a fellow we should neuer speake but at a stile, a gate, or a ditch, where a man can go no further. I was once at a Comedie in Cambridge, and there I saw a parasite make faces and mouths of all sorts on this fashion.[2]

A guide to what happened on the stage is sometimes given in warnings against too theatrical an 'action'. Thus Fraunce declares that 'the clapping of the hands is fitter for the stage than the court'.[3] And Bulwer agrees in denouncing the 'artificiall plauditie of the hand'. He sees this 'Manuall plausibilitie' as a gesture 'too plebeian & Theatrically light for the *Hands* of any prudent Rhetorician'.[4] Of shaking the arms 'with a kinde of perpetuall motion, as if they would straightway flie out of the sight of their Auditours', he says: 'This gesture is most proper to Mimiques, and the Theater; and can scarce stand with the gravitie of the Forum, or the reverence of the Church; unlesse some part of it well moderated, may be permitted in signification of Gladnes of heart.'[5] Again, 'The trembling *Hand* is scenicall,

[1] Ibid.
[2] *The Return from Parnassus*, IV. iii.
[3] Op. cit., sig. K3ᵛ.   [4] *Chiron.*, pp. 105–7.   [5] Ibid., pp. 113–15.

and belongs more to the theater, then the forum.'[1] Aware that 'to touch the breast with the *Hand*', may easily degenerate into a theatrical gesture, he debates 'whether it be convenient'. Some, he declares, 'would have the *Hand* to be onely turned, and so referred to the Breast'. But the weight of Cresollius' opinion, always to be respected, was added to that of the experts who would let a speaker touch the chest lightly with the finger-tips,

when we speake any thing concerning our selves, and that our speech glydes with a calme and gentle streame. But the touch doth most availe in a sharpe and inflamed stile, when the motions of the minde are by Action unfolded: As when an Oratour would expresse an incredible ardour of love lodged in his bosome, and cleaving to his very marrow; or griefe deeply setled in his yearning bowells; in signifying these and such like affections, none can rebuke an Oratour if he shal touch his Breast with his *Fingers* ends only. *Cresollius* makes little doubt, but *Tully* used this gesture, when he said, *miserum me &c.* for in such occasions, the splendour of pronunciation is lacking, neither have words sufficient force to make the minde altogether intelligible, unlesse the *Hand* be brought to the Breast.[2]

Bulwer treats this gesture again, among the Canons of the Rhetoricians concerning the Hands:

The Breast stricken with the *Hand*, is an action of *Griefe, sorrow, repentance*, and *indignation*. This is a very patheticall motion in Nature, & Rhetorical in Art; an action in use with the ancient Oratours, and with a profitable signification practised by the Jesuits.[3]

Nevertheless, he calls for extreme caution in its use:

Which Rhetoricall action of the *Hand* is not alwaies (to an inch) framed by the precepts of Rhetoricians, nor by line and levell fitted to the rule of Art, nor weighed, as 'twere, in the Goldsmiths ballance; for they who assume this gesture, strike their breast with an audible stroake, when they judge it fit for their purpose; although some, who are more studious of eloquence, doe not heartily admit of this loud contact of the Hand; who with a peaceable meeknesse bringing the quiet Hand unto the breast, by the forcible atchievements of that pro-

---

[1] *Chiron.* p. 104.   [2] Ibid., pp. 39–40.   [3] Ibid., p. 46.

nunciation, procure a dreadfull influence to fall upon their Auditory. But in a Senate of the Learned, and a solemne Assembly of venerable personages, a vehement percussion of the breast is not convenient; but is to be remitted to the Theater lest (as my Author saith) some Stripling in Eloquence, should tacitely throw at them out of the Comœdie;

Hic pectus digitis pultat, cor credo evocaturus foras.[1]

Whilst modern taste prefers the 'quiet hand', there is clearly a possibility that the first Hamlet may have procured 'a dreadfull influence' to fall upon his audience by means of a 'vehement percussion' or 'an audible stroake' when the opening lines of the first soliloquy were pronounced. Bulwer deals with the gesture yet again among the notes entitled 'Prevarications': 'To bring the *Fingers* ends to the Breast, the *Hand* hollow, when we speake to our selves, or in cohortation, objurgation, or commiseration, is an action that will seldome become the *Hand* of an Oratour; or to strike the breast with the *Hand*, which is Scenicall,'[2]. In the theatre, 'The Forehead stricken with the *Hand*, is an action of *dolour*, *shame*, and *admiration*'.[3] But Bulwer, following Cresollius, dislikes it: 'my Author concurres in opinion with *Quintilian*, and adjudgeth it worthy of banishment from the Hand of an Oratour, and to be confined to the Theater, and the ridiculous Hands of Mimicks.'[4] According to Canon XVIII,·

The shewing forth of the *Hand*, or beckning with the same, are Rhetorically significant to *speake* to, *call after*, *invite*, *bring in*, and *warne to come.*

But Cresollius demanded restraint,

and would have *invitations* signified by putting forth the *Hand* onely, without any waving motion; for, that Beckning with the Hand, in his judgement, is the propertie of an unskilfull multitude, and of men of small account, who want gravitie and moderation; who doe not onely induce and apply their bent-in-Hand to this *perswasive* behaviour, but doe also revoke and bow back their whole body, and wind and wrest about their very sides: Who though he doe not forbid or repudiate this *calling* gesture of the *Hand* alone, yet if the body be

---

[1] Ibid., pp. 46–7.   [2] Ibid., p. 103.   [3] Ibid., p. 47.   [4] Ibid., p. 50.

drawne in withall, he would have it referr'd to the Stage, and to places of common resort.[1]

When Shakespeare played the frowning majesty of the Ghost on the stage in a 'place of common resort', he had every justification for refusing to invite Hamlet to go with him with any courtesy beyond that of the 'bent-in-Hand'.

Next to the difference involved in suiting the action to the word, the great distinction between the acting of orators and stage-players seems to have been in the matter of style. Even when each used the same gesture the orator was less flamboyant or, as the renaissance has it, less 'vehement' than the player. Wright, who, it will be recalled, tells us that in 'the substance of externall action for most part' they agreed, adds, 'and onely they differ in this, that these act fainedly, those really'. And whilst the orator, who acts 'really', does so to persuade, 'to stirre vp all sorts of passions according to the exigencie of the matter,' the player, who acts 'fainedly', does so in the performance of a fiction, 'onely to delight'. In addition, actors 'intermingle much leuitie in their action to make men laugh', but orators 'vse all grauitie, grace, and authoritie to persuade: wherefore these are accounted rediculous, those esteemed prudent'.[2] The closer our study of the actual details of rhetorical delivery becomes, the more apparent is it that we are justified in accepting the conclusions advanced in Chapter I. A note in Wright's margin refers to Book III of Cicero's *De Oratore*, where the same relationship between acting and oratory is shown to have existed in ancient Rome as in Elizabethan England. And the awareness of the relationship permeated Elizabethan civilization to such an extent that Bulwer was by no means idiosyncratic when, to maintain '*the necessitie & dignitie of this art of* MANUALL RHETORICK', he declared:

How prevalent Gestures accommodated to perswade, have ever been in the *Hand*; both the Ancient Worthies, as also Use and daily Experience make good, it being a thing of greater moment then the vulgar thinke, or are able to judge of: which is not onely confined to

---

[1] *Chiron.*, pp. 40–1.   [2] Op. cit., p. 179.

Schooles, Theaters, and the Mansions of the Muses; but doe apper-
taine to Churches, Courts of Commonpleas, and the Councell-Table;
where we daily see many admirable things done by those, who in the
course of Humanitie and profitable studies, have been well instructed
and inform'd in this facultie of the *Hand*.[1]

Certainly those who were responsible for the First Folio version
of *Titus Andronicus* seem to have agreed with Bulwer: for in the
scene to which I have already referred, they put into the mouth
of Titus the following question:

> How can I grace my talke,
> Wanting a hand to giue it action.

[1] *Chiron.*, sig. A6r.

IV

THE RHETORICAL PRONUNCIATION AND GESTURE FIT FOR EVERY WORD, SENTENCE, AND AFFECTION

IN this chapter I propose to consider the importance of Kempe's direction that children should be taught 'the Rhetoricall pronounciation and gesture fit for every word, sentence, and affection'. For in this statement lies the key to the Elizabethan actor's ability to perform plays that were good 'theatre' without prejudice to their qualities as literature. Kempe was referring to full pronunciation as consisting of two elements, which are inseparably fused in practice, although they can be distinguished in theoretical analysis and in the exercise needed to perfect technique. By declaiming his lines with the action fit for every word and sentence the Elizabethan player ensured that the audience could experience the words heard in the theatre in the manner that literature is experienced from the printed page. And his use of the 'pronunciation and gesture' fit for every affection enabled him to represent emotion naturally and vigorously enough to satisfy the tastes of a popular audience. This much is clear from renaissance works on rhetorical delivery.

The first of these two elements in *actio* is described by Wright as 'to act aptly,' with the comment that it consists 'in a certaine moderation of the voice and qualifications of gesture'.[1] The technique depended for its success on the ability of the speaker to pay due attention both to the exact quality of each individual word, and to the effect which is to be achieved by the combination making up the phrase, the sentence, and the period. The writer of MS. Ashmole 768 tells us, therefore, that in the 'ordering' of the voice, regard must be had not only to single words but also to whole sentences.[2] And Fraunce supports him: 'The consideration of voyce is to be had either in seuered words,

---

[1] Op. cit., p. 172. [2] *MS. Ashmole 768*, p. 540.

or in the whole sentence.'[1] Before, however, a speaker can be certain how to treat an individual word he must be able to recognize, or he must have had explained to him, the part it plays in the structure of figures and tropes, which were often described as 'ornament poeticall'.

Renaissance rhetoricans speak of three kinds of ornament: tropes, figures of words, and figures of thought, these latter sometimes being described as figures of 'affection' or 'passionate figures'. Puttenham observes that 'the learned clerks who haue written methodically of this Arte in the two master languages, Greeke and Latine, haue sorted all their figures into three rankes, and the first they bestowed vpon the Poet onely, the second vpon the Poet and Oratour indifferently, the third vpon the Oratour alone.' He puts figures of words in his first category, remarking that this 'first sort of figures doth serue th'eare onely and may be therefore called *Auricular*': next come tropes, which he calls 'sensable' figures, serving 'the conceit onely and not th'eare': and last he puts the figures of thought, declaring: 'your third sort serues as well th'eare as the conceit, and may be called *sententious figures*, because not only they properly apperteine to full sentences, for bewtifying them with a currant & pleasant numerositie, but also giuing them efficacie and enlarging the whole matter besides with copious amplifications.'[2]

Although Puttenham remarks that the ancients had bestowed the third sort of figures 'vpon the Oratour alone', he nevertheless directs that his Poet or maker should use all three; and indeed it is difficult to understand how the ancient distinction can have any force outside the domain of theoretical analysis; poets always have made use, and no doubt always will continue to make use of each kind of figure, just so long as each is involved in the expression of the exact blend of thought and emotion in the poet's mind, of which the poem is born. And this holds good of dramatic poetry as of any other kind, as we can see for our-

[1] Op. cit., sig. H7[r].
[2] *The Art of English Poesy* (1589), ed. G. D. Willcock and A. Walker (1936), pp. 159–60.

selves, either by an independent analysis, or by turning to those which renaissance critics and writers of school-editions have made of the plays of the ancients and of their own later age. For our purposes here it is best to adopt Puttenham's broader division in the third chapter of Book III.

This ornament then is of two sortes, one to satisfie & delight th'eare onely by a goodly outward shew set vpon the matter with wordes, and speaches smothly and tunably running: another by certaine intendments or sence of such wordes & speaches inwardly working a stirre to the mynde: that first qualitie the Greeks called *Enargia*, of this word *argos*, because it geueth a glorious lustre and light. This latter they called *Energia* of *ergon*, because it wrought with a strong and vertuous operation; and figure breedeth them both, some seruing to giue glosse onely to a language, some to geue it efficacie by sence, and so by that meanes some of them serue th'eare onely, some serue the conceit onely and not th'eare: there be of them also that serue both turnes as common seruitours appointed for th' one and th' other purpose.[1]

It was the business of the Elizabethan actor to make certain that both the *Enargia* and the *Energia* of his author's lines were able to exert their full effect upon the audience in the theatre. And an understanding of what this technique involved is most easily gained by turning to the directions given in the rhetoric books for the correct pronunciation, first of figures of words, and then of tropes and figures of thought.

According to Fraunce, figures of words 'altogether consist in sweete repetitions and dimensions', in the pronouncing of which is 'chiefly conuersant that pleasant and delicate tuning of the voyce, which resembleth the consent and harmonie of some well ordred song'.[2] That, of course, is why Puttenham spoke of them as 'auricular'. The same doctrine is still being expressed as late as 1676 in a work on rhetoric translated from the French, *The Art of Speaking*. Here we are told that 'in repeating the same words, there are ways of disposing them with such art, that answering one another, they make an excellent Cadence, and are very

---

[1] Ibid., pp. 142-3.   [2] Op. cit., sig. H7^r.

pleasing to the Ear. These are called harmonious Repetitions.'[1]
In the same work the statement is made that 'the Study and Art
that appear in a compt and polite Discourse, are not the Character of a Mind lively touch'd with the things of which he speaks,
but rather of a Man unconcern'd and merry. So we call these
Figures of Measure, whose Cadence is agreeable to the Ear,
Theatrical Figures, Theatrales Figuræ.[2]

Rhyme is a figure of words much used by Elizabethan dramatists, who could rely on their actors to make it distinctive both
in stichomythia and at the end of acts and scenes. And in these
latter cases a quality must have been conferred on the couplets
not unlike that of a full-close in opera. Moreover, just as a theme
or motif can be stressed musically in opera, so in Elizabethan
drama it was possible by the use of rhyme to emphasize a theme
or motif poetically. It was for this reason that Samuel Daniel
insisted that rhyme should be used in tragedy 'where a sentence
shall require a couplet'.[3] The Elizabethans were accustomed to
the employment of 'sentence' or *sententia* to hint at a motif
underlying a scene, or to sum up and stress the theme of a play,
or the implications involved in the development of part of a
play. When the *sententia* was itself expressed in rhyme, the
actor who knew how to 'tune' his voice correctly was able to
ensure that the important words stood out from their context to
receive the understanding attention of the audience.

At school the Elizabethan was instructed in the use of *sententia*
in every kind of writing, and particularly in tragedy. Erasmus
deals with the problem of welding this and other figures into a
theme so that their function is more than ornamental.[4] And
Scaliger explains how to use *sententiae* in tragedy:

When a sentiment has two modes of expression, the tragedy throughout is to rest upon each, for together they constitute, as it were, a
sustaining column or pillar for the entire structure. A sentiment may
be put simply and definitely, as when we say, 'Death makes the good

---

[1] *The Art of Speaking* (1676), p. 107 (sig. H7ʳ).
[2] *Ibid.*, pp. 145–6 (sigs. L1ʳ–L1ᵛ).
[3] S. Daniel, *A Defence of Rhyme*, ed. Gregory Smith, op. cit., ii. 382.
[4] *De Ratione Studii*, tr. T. W. Baldwin, op. cit., i. 88–9.

happy,' or it may be expressed figuratively at greater length, as when
the above sentiment is thus expressed: 'Be not willing to think of
good men as perishing, whose souls, *per se* immortal, take their flight
from out these miseries to those seats whence they had departed.'
A sentiment may also be relieved of its plainness by being put into
the mouth of some person; thus Socrates is made to speak in the
Apology and in the *Phaedo*.[1]

Shakespeare has not only used *sententiae* in the manner described by Scaliger, but has also expressed them in couplets as
advocated by Daniel. Lady Macbeth, beginning to realize the
consequences of the crimes in which she has shared, proclaims
(III. ii.):

> Nought's had, all's spent,
> Where our desire is got without content:
> 'Tis safer, to be that which we destroy,
> Then by destruction dwell in doubtfull ioy.

Rhyme draws the attention of the audience to these two 'sentences'; and their force is felt even more deeply when Macbeth
himself admits with bitterness some moments later:

> Better be with the dead,
> Whom we, to gayne our peace, haue sent to peace,
> Then on the torture of the Minde to lye
> In restlesse extasie.

Here the dramatist has achieved what we call a 'dramatic effect'
by taking advantage of the actor's ability to pronounce figures
of words with the 'pleasant delicate tuning of the voice' to which
Fraunce refers.

Again, in *Hamlet*, the same technique is used, once before
and once after the play-scene has revealed Claudius' guilt. The
first example occurs at the end of the third scene of Act I, when
Hamlet has resolved to watch on the battlements for the Ghost
which resembles his father:

> foule deeds will rise,
> Though all the earth orewhelm them to mens eies.

These words are a comment on the first half of the play, a forecast of what is going to happen, as well as an assurance that it

---

[1] J. C. Scaliger, *Poetics: Select Translations* by F. M. Padelford (1905),
pp. 59–60.

always does happen. The second half of the play is similarly illuminated by the words which Gertrude speaks whilst waiting for the entry of Ophelia (IV. iii):

> To my sicke soule (as sinnes true Nature is)
> Each toy seemes Prologue, to some great amisse,
> So full of Artlesse iealousie is guilt,
> It spill's it selfe, in fearing to be spilt.

Such uses of *sententia* by a dramatist may seem unfamiliar to us, but they were the commonplace of the Elizabethan school-room, where dramatic texts were handled according to the methods of Vives and Erasmus. And how thorough such treatment could be is exemplified by an annotated edition like Pals-grave's *Acolastus*.[1] Moreover, an exchange of dialogue between Portia and Nerissa at the beginning of *The Merchant of Venice* suggests that a certain formality was associated with the pronouncing of 'sentences', even when they were not couched in verse. In her own way as melancholy as Antonio in the previous scene, Portia sighs fretfully (I. ii): 'By my troth *Nerissa*, my little body is a wearie of this great world.' To which Nerissa answers: 'You would be sweet Madam, if your miseries were in the same abundance as your good fortunes are: and yet for ought I see, they are as sicke that surfet with too much, as they that starue with nothing; it is no smal happinesse therefore to bee seated in the meane, superfluitie comes sooner by white haires, but competencie liues longer.' And Portia comments: 'Good sentences, and well pronounc'd.'

The Elizabethan liking for *sententia* is easily explained. The figure enabled a poet to relate the universal to the particular with an impressive elegance which contributed to the majesty and elevated tone of tragedy. Minturno tells us that by means of 'sentences' a poet can give majesty and beauty to his work.[2] Cinthio believed that although Seneca's style might with advantage have been more chaste in some respects, he nevertheless

---

[1] See, for instance, the 'Obseruation of the Rhetorical composition vsed by the auctour in this sceane nexte ensuynge' (IV. i), op. cit., pp. 145 ff.

[2] *L'Arte Poetica* (1564), pp. 287–8.

surpassed the Greeks in his majestic and skilful use of *sententia*: and, like Daniel, this Italian playwright-critic advised the employment of rhyme to ensure the understanding attention of the audience.[1] And Ben Jonson's apology for the deficiencies of *Sejanus* applied to popular drama as a whole, in so far as he named 'fulnesse and frequencie of Sentence' as one of the 'offices of a *Tragick* writer'.[2] Similarly, Chapman justified *The Revenge of Bussy d'Ambois* as constituting in part an 'elegant and sententious excitation to Vertue'.[3]

In addition to ornament, perspicuity is a quality of style whose value is stressed by the rhetoricians; and 'apt' action could be used to maintain perspicuity in declamation. Thus we are told by Bulwer: 'The Eare *Finger* appearing erect out of a bended Fist, doth by that action obtain a force to explaine more subtill things.'[4] With this use of the 'Eare', or little finger, Hamlet might have concentrated attention on the subtlety of 'there's the rub' (see 'T', Fig. 6). Ulysses in *Troilus and Cressida* might easily have been depicted by an actor using the impressive 'gesture of Rhetoricall *asseveration*', which involves 'the *Hand* brought to the stomacke, and spread gently thereon'.[5] And I see no reason why, the correct circumstances often occurring, the actors should not often have used the right hand in the following manner described in *Chironomia*:

The top of the *Fore-finger* moved to joyne with the naile of the *Thumbe* that's next unto it, the other fingers in remitter, is opportune for those who *relate*, *distinguish*, or *approve*. 'Tis also fit for them that *mildly councell*, and becomes the phrases of *pompous Elocution*, with which *Rhetoricians* polish and enrich their Orations. 'Tis seasonable also for *Narrations* and *Panegyriques*, where a soft & pellucid Oration flowes with the copious streames of Eloquence, and it availes in any *painted kinde of speech*, and agrees with an *Epidixis*.[6]

If 'action' was important in giving what Puttenham calls 'efficacie' to figures of words, it was no less important for tropes

---

[1] *Discorsi* (1554), pp. 220, 234.
[2] Ed. Herford and Simpson, iv. 350.
[3] 1613 ed., sig. A3ᵛ.
[4] *Chiron.*, p. 83.   [5] Ibid., p. 39.   [6] Ibid., pp. 73–4.

and figures of thought. According to MS. Ashmole 768, the voice was to be regulated in such a way

in single wordes that everie one haue his intencion according to his signification, wherevppon the kindes of Tropes (if they bee of force) may appeare. ffor noe otherwise can an Ironie, and a metaphore be made more manifest and sett forthe more effectuall.

In the whole sentence alsoe there is a certaine orderinge and disposing of the voice wherein the figures of garnishing the speach and the affections are spetiallie seene.[1]

Again Fraunce agrees:

In the particular applying of the voyce to seuerall words, wee make tropes that bee most excellent plainly appeare. For without this change of voyce, neither anie *Ironia*, nor liuely *Metaphore* can well bee discerned.

By that kinde of voyce which belongeth to whole sentences, all kindes of figures and passionate ornaments of speach are made manifest.[2]

And the Italian, Bonifaccio, who has already been mentioned, remarks that

there are taught by the rhetoricians many figures called by them schemes and tropes: which consist more in signs than in words: which ornament and embellish the oration marvellously. Such is Irony, in which through showing itself by means of gesture exactly the opposite of what is pronounced with the voice, the desire is that the listeners will believe the gesture and not the voice.[3]

He mentions other figures: 'Micterismo', 'Aganactesi', 'Enfasi', —this is 'a silent strength, and adds exceedingly to the meaning of the words',—and 'Energia . . . which by means of gesture adds vigour to the things which are being pronounced'. He ends: 'and there are many others, which for brevity I shall not treat of now.'

Among his 'sensable figures', or tropes, Puttenham, too, mentions '*Micterismus*', or 'a fleering frumpe'.[4] And Bulwer tells us how to act it: 'To present the index and eare-finger wagging,

---

[1] MS. Ashmole 768, p. 540.
[2] Op. cit., sig. H7r.
[3] Bonifaccio, op. cit., p. 552.
[4] Op. cit., p. 191.

with the Thumb applied unto the temples, is their expression
who would scornfully reprove.' He adds, that

hence comes your scornfull frumpe and drie scoffe, keen jeers that
wit hath turned up trump, wherein the dealer rubbeth with a gibe,
making another his laughing stocke; which cunning game is received
into Rhetoricke, and called an Ironie, a Trope, which gives a man
leave closely to carpe at the manners of men, wherein that which is
expressed by words, the contrary is shewn by the gesture.[1]

It seems a suitable accompaniment for the immortal 'Blesse thee
Bottome, blesse thee; thou art translated!'

What Puttenham says of figurative language in general is
especially applicable to figures of thought: they constitute a
'noueltie of language euidently (and yet not absurdly) estranged
from the ordinarie habite and manner of our dayly talke and
writing'.[2] This is also the teaching of the *Art of Speaking*:
'These ways of Speaking (which are Characters drawn by our
Passions in our Discourse) are the famous *Figures* mentioned
by Rhetoricians, and by them defin'd, *Manners of Speaking,
different and remote from the ways that are ordinary and natural.*'[3]
As with tropes, so with figures of thought, the body was used
to supplement the effect of the voice. Antithesis, which, by
'opposition of contrary things, contributes exceedingly to the
clearing of a Truth',[4] obviously needs a 'moderation' of the voice
to draw attention to the key words in relation to the rest of the
text, and to one another. And Bulwer gives a suitable gesture:
'If both *Hands* by turnes behave themselves with equall Art,
they fitly move to set off any matter that goes by way of *Antithesis* or *opposition.*'[5]

The hands could be used in this way when the speaker is
announcing the two alternatives of an Addubitation (see 'P' in
Fig. 5), bringing them together in the action which Bulwer calls
Addubitabit, and which has already been described.[6] Thus
Hamlet could extend his right hand for the words, 'To be',

[1] *Chirol.*, pp. 181–3.   [2] *Op. cit.*, p. 159.
[3] *The Art of Speaking*, p. 94 (sig. G7^v).
[4] Ibid., p. 136 (sig. K4^v).   [5] *Chiron.*, p. 58.
[6] See *supra*, pp. 44–5.

whilst the left with a negative, repulsing gesture sets off 'or not to be'. The two hands could then be brought together for the deliberative pose which states 'that is the question'. (See 'X' in Fig. 5.) It is true that these are the mechanics and not the soul of acting; nevertheless, it was necessary to be trained in such stylized methods of 'pronouncing' the text in order to recognize, even before trying to communicate, the force of oppositions to an audience. For instance, in the opening three lines of the sonnet in which Romeo and Juliet first speak to one another (I.v), the success of an antithesis depends on the ability of the actor to stress the fact that Romeo offers the alternative of his 'lips' in addition to the unworthy 'hand' which may be rejected.

In so far as figures of thought are 'Characters drawn by our Passions in our Discourse', it is obvious that they required an emotional manner of declamation. Even to-day when asking a question we elevate the voice. But in Shakespeare's time both hand and voice could be used to pronounce this figure. Bulwer remarks that, although from one point of view it is impossible to mime question with the hand in dumbshow, 'yet commonly when wee *demand*, however it be composed, we use to change or turne our *hand*, raising it a little upwards'.[1] When question was used to express powerful emotion, as with Macbeth's so famous 'Is this a dagger?' the gesture must have been more urgent.

As soon as we consider how far emotion was to be represented in order to pronounce the 'passionate' figures correctly, we see clearly that in practice there could have been no hard and fast division between the technique required for 'every word and sentence' and what was needed for 'every affection'. It will be remembered that Brinsley spoke of exercises given by Butler and Talaeus, which should be used to teach the boys how to pronounce such figures as *Exclamation*, *Apostrophe*, and *Prosopopeia*. Whilst it was necessary to pronounce in such a way that the listeners could respond to the rhetorical figure, an element of miming was no less essential. And as a result the rhetoricians have much to say on the representation of emotions which can

[1] *Chiron.*, p. 37.

help us to re-create the atmosphere of an Elizabethan performance.

Rhetorical doctrine on the miming of the passions is well
represented by Wright. In a paragraph headed *How Passions are
moued by action*, he declares:

> We said aboue, that externall actions as voice, and gestures, were
> signes of internall passions; and there we taught, how thorow those
> windowes a man might passe with the sight of his vnderstanding,
> and discouer the secret affections of anothers heart: the which ground
> and vndoubted veritie, is the foundation whereupon now we must
> build this third meane to moue passions: for *Cicero* expressly teacheth
> that it is almost impossible for an oratour to stirre vp a passion in his
> auditors, except he be first affected with the same passion himselfe.[1]

That was why Wright not only advised the orator to watch men
'appassionat', but told him also to notice 'how they demeane
themselues in passions, and obserue what and how they speak in
mirth, sadnesse, ire, feare, hope, &c. what motions are stirring in
the eyes, hands, bodie, &c.'[2]

Since the time of Aristotle the study of rhetoric had included
a treatment of the emotions. This was logical for two reasons: if
we restrict the subject for the moment to cover no more than the
use of words in persuasive oratory, the study of the emotions is
still included in so far as the orator has to use them to attain his
end: on the other hand, if we regard rhetoric as the subject
which teaches all kinds of composition, it is no less true that the
poet and playwright must know the 'springs' of the human
mind, how to evoke and how to express the emotions, whilst
understanding, too, the need to take into account distinctions of
age and rank. The dramatist, no less than the orator, studies the
passions as part of the training which enables him to treat what
Aristotle, followed by the renaissance critics, called *thought*.[3]
Moreover, they, like their master, held that the poet must turn
to the experts on rhetoric in order to learn how to compose
thought and emotion into words.

The dramatist and his performers benefited from the long

---

[1] Op. cit., p. 172.　　　　　　　　　[2] Ibid., p. 179.
[3] Aristotle, *On the Art of Poetry*, trans. Bywater, pp. 66–7.

tradition which led Thomas Wright to stress the importance of emotion, in words which represent accurately the normal opinions of those who taught rhetoric:

It cannot be that he which heareth should sorrow, hate, enuie, or feare any thing, that he should be induced to compassion or weeping, except all those motions the oratour would stirre vp in the iudge, be first imprinted and marked in the oratour himselfe. . . . Furthermore the passion passeth not onely thorow the eyes, but also pierceth the eare, and thereby the heart; for a flexible and pliable voice, accommodated in manner correspondent to the matter whereof a person intreateth, conueyeth the passion most aptly, pathetically, and almost harmonically, and euery accent, exclamation, admiration, increpation, indignation, commiseration, abhomination, exanimation, exultation, fitly (that is distinctly, at time and place, with gesture correspondent, and flexibilitie of voice proportionat) deliuered, is either a flash of fire to incense a passion, or a bason of water to quench a passion incensed.[1]

The same point of view is put by Bulwer, though more soberly: 'for, all men (a thing nature hath so appointed) are stirred & moved by the same motives of the mind, and doe in others understand and take notice of the same moving demonstrations, by experience judging and approving in themselves those affections that outwardly appeare to worke upon others.'[2]

Henry V's invocation to imitate 'the action of the Tyger', shows that actors on the stage were trying, at least, to perform the 'actions' prescribed in academic works on rhetoric, psychology, physiology, and related subjects. There, too, we are told that rage and anger lend the eye 'a terrible aspect', to which even greater force is added by the menace of an overhanging brow. The frown is so firmly associated with anger that Hamlet asks if the ghost looked 'frowningly'. But Horatio is quick to point out that the general appearance was more sorrowful than angry. The ghost evidently did not create the impression which makes Cranmer say in *Henry VIII* (v. i):

> I am fearefull: Wherefore frownes he thus?
> 'Tis his Aspect of Terror.

[1] Op. cit., pp. 172–5.   [2] *Chiron.*, p. 4.

In the next scene of this play the nobles trying the Archbishop are struck with terror by Henry's entrance '*frowning on them*'. Earlier, Wolsey expresses his dismay at the behaviour of Henry towards him, which is described in a stage direction as '*Exit King, frowning upon the Cardinall*' (III. ii).

We are told more about rage in a passage which seems to be the result of Thomas Wright's careful observation, if not of his personal experience.

The manner of this action wee may best discouer in wittie women when they chide; because although their excesse be vitious and not to be imitated, yet for that they let nature worke in her kind, their furious fashion will serue for a good meane to perceiue the externall manage of this passion. Their voyce is loud and sharpe, and consequently apt to cut, which is proper to ire and hatred, which wish ill, and intend reuenge: their gestures are frequent, their faces inflamed, their eyes glowing, their reasons hurry one in the necke of another, they with their fingers number the wrongs offered them, the harmes, iniuries, disgraces, and what not, thought sayd, and done against them: if a prudent oratour could in this case better their matter, circumcise the weaknesse of the reason, abate the excesse of their furie, certainlie he might win a pretie form for framing his action.[1]

But the stage-player, who was not bound by the same considerations of 'prudence', could indulge in the violence denied to the orator, especially when playing a role such as that of Hotspur, or Hamlet in the 'Hecuba' soliloquy. Bulwer tells us: 'The Right *Index*, if it Marshal-like goe from *Finger* to *Finger*, to note them out with a light touch, it doth fit their purpose who would *number their arguments*, and by a visible distinction set them all on a row upon their *Fingers*.'[2] This is a fitting action for Hamlet as he counts, 'Remorseless, treacherous, lecherous, kindless, villain': and the violence of the last word is succeeded by an even more overwhelming climax, in which the time normally given to ten syllables is allotted to the long-drawn-out howl of 'O, vengeance!' which is given in the First Folio version. Another gesture to be used in a heated argument is described thus: 'The middle joynt of the left *Index* apprehended, intends more

[1] Op. cit., pp. 180–1.   [2] *Chiron.*, p. 83.

earnestnes, and sublimates the sense of words unto a point of greater *vehemencie*.'[1]

In the plays of *Henry VI* and *Richard III*, Queen Margaret has speeches in which such signs of rage as stamping the feet are suitable, in addition to those described by Wright. Her character calls for the gesture which Bulwer describes as 'To put the fingers into a gripe or claw-like aspect, and to scratch or claw another therewith'.[2] Other signs of anger are the hand striking the thigh, and the right fist struck against the open left palm to produce a startling noise. Sometimes anger was shown as of the dangerous smouldering kind, which burns quietly underground, whilst the 'person of the drama' in his 'outer show' seems rather reserved and abstracted, turned in on himself, in a silent distraction which can, as with Hamlet at the beginning of the play, suggest either grief or love. Aaron, in *Titus Andronicus*, therefore explains to Tamora that his appearance of abstraction is not that of the lover, but of one who quietly contemplates revenge.

Another sign of deep contemplation is provided by the 'wreathed arms', which are so often mentioned in connexion with melancholy. When the arms are folded they symbolize inexpressiveness to an age accustomed to regarding hand and arm in motion as essential to fully articulate speech. I think it is for this reason that Titus tells Marcus (III. ii):

> vnknit that sorrow-wreathen knot:
> Thy Neece and I (poore Creatures) want our hands
> And cannot passionate our tenfold griefe,
> With foulded Armes.

Whilst they feel more than a dull grief, their mutilations do not allow the expression of what is really within. Conversely, in Hamlet's sorrow, it is the combination of frowning, silence, and folded arms that calls forth rebuke for too passionate an expression of an inward grief, so intense that it allows no sign of interest in the affairs of the world around him. And in this case we are told that Hamlet has 'that within which passeth' even this

[1] Ibid., p. 75.   [2] *Chirol.*, p. 181.

very expressive show. What suits one kind of grief is in every respect unsuitable to the other. If Lavinia's hands had not been cut off she would probably have wrung them in the manner described by Bulwer (see *Ploro*, 'C' in Fig. 2). 'To wring the hands is a naturall expression of *excessive griefe*, used by those who *condole, bewaile*, and *lament*.' He now tells us that, according to Bacon,

sorrow which diminisheth the body it affects, provokes by wringing of the minde, teares, the sad expressions of the eyes; which are produced and caused by the contraction of the spirits of the Braine, which contraction doth straine together the moisture of the Braine, constraining thereby teares into the eyes; from which compression of the Braine proceeds the hard wringing of the hands, which is a Gesture of expression of moysture.

This 'compectination or weeping crosse of the *Hand*' is 'the declaration of a mind *languishing for grief*, and *almost spent, and wearied with some vehement affliction*'.[1] It is the 'action' used by Gertrude in the Closet Scene (III. iv), prompting her son to bid 'Leaue wringing of your hands', and, as she sits down, he wrings his own with more purpose, and with a different intensity, suiting the words 'and let me wring your heart'.

An appreciation of the Elizabethan *Hamlet* depends upon our awareness of the individual significances attached to different kinds of 'actions'. Because the frown is the sign not only of anger, but also of grief and love, the Prince's appearance must be a puzzle to those who have reason to suppose him subject to all or any of the three. For where Polonius diagnoses love, Gertrude finds grief; and they are therefore more of a hindrance than an aid to Claudius apprehensive of what the second Quarto (III. iii) calls the

> Hazerd so neer's as doth hourely grow
> Out of his browes.

This reading makes good sense in the light of Elizabethan acting. Scowling and frowning belong to the 'action' of Hamlet on the Elizabethan stage. And a point has been reached at which

[1] *Chirol.*, pp. 28–9.

Claudius is rightly apprehensive; even if he is not certain of the reason for their 'bending', these 'browes' suggest that an act of violence is contemplated against him.

According to renaissance psychology, anatomy, and physiology the attraction of humours towards the heart, as a result of excessive emotions, subjected it to a physical strain. The sigh of the melancholy man literally eased his heart; but the normal urge of a person feeling strong emotions was to give them full expression by means of language, hands, face, and body. Restraint was dangerous now; although, earlier, it would have meant the avoidance or diminution of the passion. Thus Malcolm exclaims to Macduff (IV. iii): 'Giue sorrow words.' And he adds warningly:

> the griefe that do's not speake,
> Whispers the o're-fraught heart, and bids it breake.

Pulling the hat over the eyes was not the only 'action' by means of which the Elizabethan player could have shown himself cast down. *Despero*, Gestus VIII in *Chirologia* (see 'H' in Fig. 2), suits this moment admirably: 'To appeare with fainting and deiected hands, is a posture of *feare*, *abasement of minde*, an *abject* and *vanquished courage*, and of utter *despaire*.'[1] Probably this was John's posture when Faulconbridge exhorts him (V. i):

> But wherefore doe you droope? why looke you sad?
> Be great in act, as you haue beene in thought.

Hamlet, however, does not show 'an abject and vanquished courage' when, with full realization of the risk to which he is deliberately subjecting himself—only one among many—he resolves: 'But break my heart—for I must hold my tongue.'

When a play was performed with rhetorical action, fit for 'euery word, sentence, and affection', the balance between the respective claims of literature, emotion, and mime was preserved by following the directions which lay for Elizabethans in the pointing of a text. Whilst we do not know exactly how this controlled *pronuntiatio*, it is certain that the relationship existed in

[1] Ibid., p. 35.

fact. The exercise known as *vociferatio* was based to some extent upon exact observance of what *The Touchstone of Complexions* calls 'stops and certayne Pauses', as was the practice of stage-players,—'our comicall fellows'.[1] It will be remembered, too, that Heywood defended acting by the observation that it was the practice at the universities to perform plays in order to learn 'with iudgement to obserue his comma's, colons, & full poynts, his parenthesis, his breathing spaces, and distinctions'.[2]

Gesture, like voice, was regulated by punctuation: Bulwer tells us that 'The *Hand* with a gentle percussion, now greater, now lesse; now flat, now sharpe, according to the diversitie of the affections, is fitted to *distinguish the Comma's & breathing parts of a sentence*'.[3] He has already been quoted to the effect that the hand was turned or 'changed' and raised upwards when asking a question.[4] This movement of the hand was designed to produce for the eye an effect parallel to that created for the ear by the elevation of voice demanded by the note of interrogation pointed in the text. A question-mark in Elizabethan printing can stand either for interrogation or exclamation; and in each case the pitch of the voice is elevated above the normal key. With a child actor, whose voice was already higher-pitched than that of a man, both question and exclamation must have produced a high, though not necessarily loud, note. Here, I believe, is a second meaning to the gibe in *Hamlet* (II. ii) at the 'little Yases, that crye out on the top of question'. To 'cry out' is, literally, to 'exclaim'. *The Arts of Logic and Rhetoric* (1584), by an anonymous author, speaks of 'a crying out, called Exclama-tion'.[5] Cockram's *Dictionary* (1637) has 'to cry out—Vociferate', and 'a crying out—Exclamation'.

To me it seems that Rosencrantz is jeering at the raising of a high-pitched child's voice on top of that normally required by a question-mark in the text. But I am not sure how far there is a conscious pun which takes advantage of the double function of this pointing: in which case he can be interpreted as saying that

---

[1] Op. cit., sigs. G5^r, G5^v.   [2] See above, p. 15.
[3] *Chiron.*, p. 44.   [4] See above, p. 69.   [5] Sig. D4^r.

they add exclamation to question, and vice versa. Sir Thomas
Wilson has a section on 'Outcrying', with a marginal note,
Exclamatio. 'Out crying, is when with voyce we make an exclamation. Oh Lord, O God, O worlde, O life, O maners of
men? O Death, where is thy sting? O Hell, where is thy victorie?'[1]
Here, it will be noticed, the exclamations are pointed with a
question; and two of them are actually rhetorical questions.

There is small hope of our understanding fully the principles
of Elizabethan punctuation until we know more about the use
of voice; in particular, how far it resembled a chant like *stilo
recitativo*. Until we know this we shall continue to be tantalized
by the accounts given in renaissance Latin grammars, and in
such English Grammars as that of Ben Jonson. Even now, however, it is clear that parenthesis conferred a different quality on
certain words and combinations from that given to those in the
rest of the speech. When, for instance, the words 'My Lord'
appear in parenthesis we are justified in envisaging the use by
the actor of both voice and body, a 'flexion' of both, in order
that his apprehension of the lordliness of his interlocutor may be
fully communicated. Charlemont refers to the change of voice
in parenthesis when, in Act I, Sc. ii of *The Atheist's Tragedy*
(1611), he asks:

> Shall I serue
> For nothing but a vaine Parenthesis,
> I' th' honour'd story of your Familie?

Prosody is more strictly the concern of what Puttenham calls
'proportion' than of 'ornament'. Nevertheless, both in prose and
verse, rhythm is a quality of style, which cannot be ignored in a
treatment of the rhetorical delivery fit for 'every word, sentence,
and affection'. There are, moreover, many indications that actors
took pains to preserve the rhythm of the lines declaimed. In *The
Touchstone of Complexions* we are told, for instance, that they
'measure rhetoricke by their peuish rhythmes'.[2] This seems to
be an attack more against the quality of the rhythms than against

---

[1] Op. cit., p. 205.   [2] Op. cit., sig. G5^{v}.

the practice of observing metre in pronunciation. Wright includes 'euerye accent' in the list of figures which are to be delivered 'fitly (that is distinctly at time and place, with gesture
correspondent, and flexibilitie of voice proportionat)'.[1] Without
embarking on the very troubled ocean of controversy as to
whether metre is properly a matter of stress, length, or accent,
we may still recognize that English renaissance prosodists use
the term 'accent'—often as a translation of *ictus*—to distinguish
between the two different kinds of syllables that go to produce
metrical feet: and this usage occurs among writers who are
aware that differences of time and length are involved, as well as
those of stress, in the writing of English verse, even if a strict
classical system of quantity is out of the question. 'But aboue
all', writes Campion, 'the accent of our words is diligently to be
obseru'd, for chiefely by the accent in any language the true
value of the sillables is to be measured.'[2] It will be remembered
that Burbage and *The Excellent Actor* were each distinguished
by knowing 'how much breath he is to give to every syllable'.
And the Knight, in the *Squire's Tale*, delivered his message,
'With-outen vyce of sillable'. It is, moreover, this very excellence which draws from the stickler, Polonius, the full-blooded
tribute, ' 'For God, my lord, well spoken, with good accent, and
good discretion'. References occur in Ben Jonson's plays to the
importance of keeping accent. Edward Knowell says of Brain-
worm:

Into the likenesse of one of these *Reformado's* had he moulded himselfe so perfectly, obseruing euery tricke of their action, as varying the
accent, swearing with an *emphasis*, indeed all, with so speciall, and
exquisite a grace, that (hadst thou seene him) thou would'st haue
sworne, he might haue beene Serieant-*Maior*, if not Lieutenant
Coronell to the regiment.[3]

In the same scene (III. v) Bobadill's facility at swearing with an

---

[1] See p. 71 above.
[2] T. Campion, *Observations in the Art of English Poesy* (1602), ed. Gregory
Smith, op. cit. ii. 351.
[3] B. Jonson, *Every Man in His Humour* (1616), ed. Herford and Simpson,
iii. 353–7.

accent and emphasis wakens the despairing envy of Stephen, who exclaims: 'Oh, he sweares admirably! (by PHARAOHS foot) (body of CAESAR) I shall neuer doe it, sure (vpon mine honor, and by Saint GEORGE) no, I ha' not the right grace.' Whereupon he proceeds to practise to the post (probably one of the pillars supporting the pent-house).

Bulwer provides information which suggests that the body also responded to the metre of declaimed verse. He has already been quoted to the effect that in one gesture the ring finger (i.e. the third) is to be extended from the open hand, 'as it were to serve the tact'.[1] He also speaks in *Chironomia* of the 'action of the hand' resembling 'the sweet cadencies of numbers'. His great authority, Cresollius, disapproved of orators using *'ictus* or musicall cadence of the fingers' in free prose, 'though it may be tollerable for the setting off the intervalls of restrained numbers'.[2] If this was allowed in oratory, it is probable that stage-players, not bound by academic restraints, suited the movements of their hands to those of the verses in their lines.

With prose an actor was obliged to recognize the important words which were to be elevated, whilst obedience to the pointing could produce a skilful and varied cadence. With verse it was necessary, in addition, to keep accent in order to preserve metre. By neglecting accent in the second syllable of a trochee, for instance, we linger and distort it into a spondee. This can ruin a line such as Hamlet's 'O, Vengeance!' or Lear's 'Never, never, never, never, never'. In both passages a dramatic effect depends upon the correct pronunciation of the metre; and in less obvious instances neglect of accent, by distorting metre, can produce a pompous, inflated style of declamation, monotonous and empty of meaning. The normally correct modulation with its variety of elevation and cadence, its meaningful inflexions of the voice according to metre, rhetorical structure, and emotion, produced what Hamlet demands from his Players, a speech pronounced 'trippingly on the Tongue'. Failure to keep

---

[1] *Chiron.*, p. 126.   [2] Ibid., pp. 122–3.

accent, stressing of unstressed or lengthening of short syllables, produces the empty, monotonous chant of the town-crier, who still to-day turns his invocation, 'Oyez', from trochee to spondee. No wonder the Prince talks of players 'that neyther hauing the accent of Christians, nor the gate of Christian, Pagan, or Norman, haue so strutted and bellowed' (III. ii). In the eighteenth century, failure to preserve the different quality distinguishing syllables in metre was referred to as 'mouthing':[1] it seems possible, in view of his insistence and that of his age on 'accent' as essential to avoid monotony, that for Shakespeare, too, to 'mouth it' was to mishandle the individual syllable of a foot so grievously that the town-crier might indeed be given the task with equal success.

Observation of 'numbers' by actors, in both voice and gesture, must have affected the tempo of individual scenes: so far as concerns stricter academic drama this seems very probable from what Ascham tells us about 'One man in Cambrige, well liked of many, but best liked of him selfe'. He had mistakenly and unskilfully begun 'the *Protasis* with *Trochoeiis Octonariis*: which kinde of verse, as it is but seldome and rare in Tragedies, so it is neuer vsed, saue onelie *in Epitasi*: whan the Tragedie is hiest and hotest and full of greatest troubles'. It was consideration for details of this kind which led Watson not to allow 'his *Absalon* to go abroad, and that onelie bicause, *in locis paribus*, *Anapestus* is twise or thrise vsed in stede of *Iambus*'.[2] The fact that the popular dramatists did not take such care would have been more apparent to a strict ear and eye than it is to-day, and explains, though without necessarily justifying, the attacks made on popular plays as bad dramatic poetry.

The question arises how far the Elizabethan audience was capable of appreciating all the refinements of technique outlined above. We hear so much of the groundlings that we are almost afraid to consider the possibility of a deliberate use by a

---

[1] T. Sheridan, *A Course of Lectures on Elocution* (1787), pp. 68–70. See also Blair, *Lectures on Rhetoric and Belles Lettres* (1783), p. 222 (note).

[2] *The Schoolmaster*, ed. cit., p. 24.

popular dramatist of a technique requiring forethought and subtlety of preparation. But the audience did not necessarily have to be capable of appreciating the subtleties of technique; a moment's consideration of the musical illiteracy of thousands of enthusiastic concert-goers is enough to convince us that it is possible to respond without understanding the technicalities of an art. The Elizabethan audience responded, not as the result of its own skill, but of that of the playwrights who knew how to use words, and of the actors who knew how to declaim them. The rhetorical technique was designed traditionally to evoke an adequate response from people who were not capable of analysing an oration or a play. We do not find it difficult to imagine that an Elizabethan audience responded to the dramatist's knowledge of prosody, however ignorant the individual ground-ling may have been of that art. And if recognition of metrical subtleties is not essential, there is no reason why we should insist on being convinced of the audience's ability to analyse dialogue into rhetorical figures, before we are prepared to believe that these same figures were used deliberately by dramatists who knew what they were doing. As long as the popular audience had not been taught artificially to expect to respond to anything but the performance of a fiction which does not pretend to be anything else, so long was there opportunity for playwright and actor to affect them by a combination of language and *actio*.

Rhetorical declamation did for the Elizabethan writer and his audiences what singing and orchestral music do for the composer and the popular audiences who flock to opera in Italy to-day. According to Bulwer: 'Men of the most obtuse understanding that are not able to conceive of the words pronounced in an unknown Tongue, to whom an Oratours spent oyle is meerly lost, because their rich and elegant expressions in conceits transcend the pitch of their capacity: yet these may see and perceive the intention of the *Hand*, which by gestures makes the inward motions of the minde most evident.'[1]

---

[1] *Chiron.*, p. 4.

It was the same acting at the disposal of the poet in the theatre which evoked from Dekker:

> Giue me *That Man*,
> Who when the *Plague* of an Impostumd *Braynes*
> (*Breaking*-out) infects a *Theater*, and hotly raignes,
> Killing the *Hearers* hearts, that the vast roomes
> Stand empty, like so many Dead-men's toombes,
> Can call the *Banishd* Auditor home, And tye
> His Eare (with golden chaines) to his Melody:
> Can draw with *Adamantine Pen*, euen creatures
> Forg'de out of th' *Hammer*, on tiptoe, to *Reach* vp,
> And (from *Rare silence*) clap their *Brawny hands*,
> T'*Applaud*, what their charm'd soule scarce vnderstands.
> That Man giue mee; whose Brest fill'd by the *Muses*,
> With Raptures, into a second, them infuses:
> Can giue an Actor, Sorrow, Rage, Ioy, Passion,
> Whilst hee againe (by self-same Agitation)
> Commands the *Hearers*, sometimes drawing out *Teares*,
> Then smiles, and fills them both with *Hopes* & *Feares*.
> That man giue mee; And to bee such a-*One*,
> Our *Poet* (this day) striues, or to bee *None*.[1]

[1] T. Dekker, *If It Be Not Good, The Devil Is In It* (1612), sig. A4[v].

V

DECORUM AND CHARACTERIZATION

IT is not always possible, nor is it always desirable, to distinguish between decorum as a social and decorum as a literary convention. To such men as Sir Thomas Elyot epic was not only a literary form; it was an inspiration for the social behaviour of virtuous men in his own day. It is clear from Book One of *The Governor* that he regarded the epics of Virgil and Homer as constituting the expression, partly by way of example, of all that makes man manlike as distinct from the animal inhabitants of this world. Whereas men of the cast of mind of Vives and Milton might deplore the example given by classical epic, as expressing the faulty ideals of a pagan culture, they agreed with Elyot that it was the business of this type of poem to illumine the mind of its readers with the consciousness of truly noble virtue. It followed naturally, both in classical times and in the renaissance, that a poem which deals with a truly noble subject must be correspondingly dignified and magnificent in style. Here the fact that the subject concerns itself with certain social conventions decides the spirit of the poem, that spirit in itself automatically deciding what can still be looked upon as the purely literary style. Decorum not only ensured that the incidents, theme, and personages should be worthy of a heroic poem; but was also responsible for complete harmony of matter and style. In popular and classical Elizabethan drama the social and more purely aesthetic elements are likewise closely intertwined.

I propose first to examine decorum as a literary, and then as a social convention, before passing on to apply the information discussed in the last four chapters to the question of character in Elizabethan plays. As a literary convention, decorum is obviously a matter of suiting subject and style. This has already been fully treated in Chapters I and II, in the first of which, it will be remembered, quotation from medieval rhetoric books established the fact that in the middle ages, too, whoever recited a poem was expected to preserve decorum of voice and countenance, if not of complete bodily gesture as well. Hamlet's direction to 'Sute the Action to the Word, the Word to the Action' (III. ii) states for the player in the theatre the same Horatian doctrine as was taught to the schoolboy and undergraduate for *actio* in the pulpit or at the bar. For player and orator alike, voice and body must function as an instrument transmitting sensitively the quality of *elocutio*, the style in which the literary record mirrored the exact quality of the subject as that existed in the author's mind. In an Italian work on the production of stage plays, *Della Poesia Rappresentativa & del Modo di Rappresentare le Favole Sceniche* (Ferrara, 1598), Angelo Ingegneri insists on the importance of the correct use of voice and body to obtain and preserve decorum: 'The perfection of every represented story depends upon decorum, which, of necessity, is created by an ordered voice and by excellence of gesture.'[1] Bulwer is even more explicit:

And indeed *Decencie* of expression doth so depend upon this Art, that (as Grammarians observe) *Decencie* is properly spoken of *Gesture*, and motions of the *Hand* and *Body*, and it so exalts Beauty from the concrete into the abstract, that Nature and the tacit voice, and assent of all men, allow of it as a thing very materiall in commerce, and is so look'd for at the *Hand* of an Orator.[2]

As soon as we apply the principle of this decorum to tragedy we find that, as in the case of epic, we have crossed over the border between a literary and a social convention. The classical doctrine of decorum in tragedy demands the perfect correspondence between subject and style which can exist in the theatre only when the actors use voice and body to communicate the spirit in which the persons represented have been imagined. As the literary conception of tragedy insists that it achieves its effects by unfolding the punishment of great crimes committed by the magnificent, the actor is at once set the task of

---

[1] A. Ingegneri, *Della Poesia Rappresentativa*, p. 77.
[2] *Chiron.*, sig. A8^v.

conveying to the audience qualities of spirit which in the Elizabethan world distinguish one class from another. Whilst the
spectators of tragedy see crime punished, they are none the less
induced to give the peculiar response which belongs to tragedy
by their apprehension of the nobility of spirit wedded to the
criminal fault or faults which render the protagonists vulnerable
to Fortune. As in epic, so in tragedy, the nobleman was ideally
a person of perfectly balanced mind, which, depending itself on
a physiological balance, was shown in all the minute details of
actio. The work of the Dutchman, Lemnius, translated into
English by Thomas Newton as *The Touchstone of Complexions*
gives us a clear account of the 'heroic' appearance, which resulted
from the balanced interplay of psychological and physiological
elements:

And not only in the inward mynd of man, do these ornamentes and
giftes of nature appeare & expressely shew out themselues, but euen in
the outward shew, shape and behauyour of the body there is euidently
descryed and perceyued a comly grace and portly dignitye. For in
the countenaunce, which is the image of the mynde, in the eyes,
which are the bewrayers and tokentellers of the inwarde conceiptes:
in the colour, lineamentes, proportion and feacture of the whole
body, ther appeareth a kind of heroicall grace and amiablenes, in so
much that the very viewe and sight therof allureth and draweth euery
one by a certayne secrete sympathy or consent of nature to loue it
without anye hope of profite or commodity therby to be reaped or
receiued.[1]

No wonder then that, in *The Tempest*, Miranda cries, 'Oh,
brave new world', at the thought of going out with her husband
and her now princely father to a world which will be, she is
assured, filled with such glorious beings. And if the producer
has expressed his author's intention, so shall we in the audience
feel that she is going out into a new world regenerated by the
grace of a Providence that is always ready to use evil to the ends
of good. The 'heroicall amiablenes' of *The Touchstone of Complexions* seems to have been known to the Elizabethan theatre;

[1] Op. cit., sigs. E4^r–E4^v.

for when Ferdinand is first seen by Miranda the glory of his 'action' is such as to draw from her the question:

> What is't a Spirit?
> Lord, how it lookes about: Beleeue me sir,
> It carries a braue forme. But 'tis a spirit.

And again:

> I might call him
> A thing diuine, for nothing naturall
> I euer saw so Noble.

The only men she has known hitherto have been her father and Caliban. And, until he discases himself as he was sometime Milan, Prospero, for all his dignity, is hardly likely to convey the same impression of nobility as is so overwhelmingly obvious in the spectacle of the young prince, his splendid clothes untouched by the sea. Caliban, on the other hand, is man almost degenerated into beast. He can hardly have been a difficult role for the Elizabethan actor; it was necessary only to give him a shambling, graceless walk, a head forever turning to the ground, so little force had the spark of reason in him to bring him erect. He frowns, he gesticulates grossly—and I would be prepared to say that on the modern stage he should never be allowed to get off the ground into the air. Anchored firmly to the earth, it is music alone that can transform him into something less brutish; and even this Shakespeare's audience would probably regard as a sign of the savage and the animal, in view of the ancient tradition that music has the unique power of swaying animals as well as man.

It is obvious that in a play such as *The Tempest*, and with a character like Ferdinand, the actor must express the noble conception of man as ideally a being of 'heroicall amiablenes'. But in tragedy the protagonists are necessarily short of the ideal standard; and it may therefore seem questionable whether the same magnificence of presence was essential. I think, however, that the nobleman, even when he was a villain, was more graceful, and more magnificent in his bearing, than the commoner. The shortcomings may have been vile; they were not petty, as

we see from the example of noble bearing fused to villainy given
us in Henry VIII's description of Buckingham (I. ii):

> The Gentleman is Learn'd, and a most rare Speaker,
> To Nature none more bound; his trayning such,
> That he may furnish and instruct great Teachers,
> And neuer seeke for ayd out of himselfe: yet see,
> When these so Noble benefits shall proue
> Not well dispos'd, the minde growing once corrupt,
> They turne to vicious formes, ten times more vgly
> Then euer they were faire. This man so compleat,
> Who was enrold 'mongst wonders; and when we
> Almost with rauish'd listning, could not finde
> His houre of speech, a minute: He, (my Lady)
> Hath into monstrous habits put the Graces
> That once were his, and is become as blacke,
> As if besmear'd in hell.

It is not surprising that the exalted view of the nature of man,
in accordance with which renaissance schooling was planned,
should have resulted in ability to speak well becoming regarded
as one of the accomplishments of the gentleman. Newton's
translation of Lemnius points out that with the mind and body
of the noble man went 'the tongue prompt and readie, distinctlye,
and sensibly able to pronounce and deliuer out his meaning
wordes of gallante vtterance'. His gesture was to be correspondingly gracious, not affected, yet 'most farre from sulleyne sterne
seuerity and Stoicall indolency'.[1]

This quality graced Shakespeare's ideal Henry V, of whom
the Archbishop says (I. i):

> when he speakes,
> The Ayre, a Charter'd Libertine, is still,
> And the mute Wonder lurketh in mens eares,
> To steale his sweet and honyed Sentences.

The difference between King and nobleman would be made
more obvious by the hedge of ceremony surrounding the monarch, to whom all would behave with the courtly 'flexure' which
the inferior accorded to those above.

[1] Op. cit., sigs. E4r–E4v.

As Elizabethan acting was designed to express the spirit through the physical medium of the body, the players were ideal instruments with which to portray the spiritual qualities which went with the different ranks, ages, and occupations of the 'persons of the drama'. In each case, in that of rank, of age, and of occupation, the distinguishing, or typifying, mark was regarded as the result of a spiritual cause; where we might see a habit of body, the Elizabethans were aware of a habit of mind, no less powerfully than such playwrights as Tchehov, although for naturalistic drama the actor must portray the behaviour of modern society, carefully avoiding the uninhibited flamboyance of the renaissance. An age which believed that monarchs 'were Gods deputies on earth' expected to see them represented with suitable magnificence, both of dress and bearing, on the stage. As early as 1563 we hear from Lawrence Humfrey: 'How hisse we oute a wel apparayled plaier, if counterfaiting a kinge on the stage, he faile of his iesture, speake yawning, haue a sower and harshe voyce, mysse his action, or vse vnseemely iesture for so stately personage?'[1] Similar demands, though with the threat of more violent penalties for failure, are made of Zanthia the slave by Corisca in Massinger's *The Bondman* (1624). Wishing to create an opportunity for her step-son to make love to her, she arranges to be imitated by the slave, to whom the man is to pay his addresses (II. ii):

> doe you heare Minion,
>
> .   .   .   .
>
> Repeat the lesson over, that I taught you
> When my young Lord came to visit me; if you misse
> In a Syllable or posture!

The 'posture' of any head of a state, whether he were King, or Duke, or Prince, would be more magnificent than that of his noblemen, unless the character resembles Mycetes in *Tamburlaine* or Arbaces in *A King and No King*. In each of these plays a deliberate attempt is made to show the monarch as unworthy in spirit of the position in which his birth or chance has placed

---

[1] L. Humfrey, *The Nobles or of Nobility* (1563), sig. x viii[r].

him. The figure of Shakespeare's Richard II is not so clear-cut. It is obvious at times that he has lost the dignity of bearing that denotes kingliness; but there are moments when his royalty flashes forth, not merely in disdain and contempt for his opponents, but in a thunderous violence which recalls the solid majesty of John of Gaunt. The behaviour of others on the stage would contribute as much as Richard's own bearing in creating a weaker or stronger impression of royalty upon the audience. From foreign accounts of life in England it is possible to imagine the complicated ceremony, with its bending of the knee and courtesies, of life at court. It was normal for subjects to remain bare-headed in the presence of their monarch; and one sign that this practice was followed on the stage is provided by Richard's words to his followers after the double blow of Scroop's message so hot on the heels of Salisbury's evil news (III. ii):

> Couer your heads, and mock not flesh and blood
> With solemne Reuerence: throw away Respect,
> Tradition, Forme, and Ceremonious dutie,
> For you haue but mistooke me all this while:
> I liue with Bread like you, feele Want,
> Taste Griefe, need Friends: subiected thus,
> How can you say to me, I am a King?

In similar circumstances King John slumps in a most unregal attitude of despair (see 'Despero', Fig. 2), calling from Faulconbridge the rebuke that one who has had kingly thoughts should allow them to keep his appearance regal in adversity (V. i):

> But wherefore doe you droope? why looke you sad?
> Be great in act, as you haue beene in thought:
> Let not the world see feare and sad distrust
> Gouerne the motion of a kinglye eye:
> Be stirring as the time, be fire with fire,
> Threaten the threatner, and out-face the brow
> Of bragging horror: So shall inferior eyes
> That borrow their behauiours from the great,
> Grow great by your example, and put on
> The dauntlesse spirit of resolution.

I do not think that Richard II ever shows fear; but he does not always maintain kingly bearing; he doubts himself as man, whilst always insisting that once anointed he is still king, even when deposed.

The behaviour of others to the King, or head of the State, is exemplified in Massinger's *The Great Duke of Florence* (1636). Cozimo enters to find his three counsellors on their knees (I. iii). One, Alphonso, tenders a written supplication to the Duke to remarry, drawing from him the expostulation:

> What needs this form? we are not grown so proud
> As to disdaine familiar conference
> With such as are to counsaile, and direct us.[1]

The Duke's affability and condescension, in the best meaning of the word, are of importance in view of the change in his be-haviour later in the play. We therefore find him refusing once more to stand on ceremony when Sanazarro enters after a few moments have passed in the same scene:

> My *Sanazarro!*—Nay,
> Forbeare all ceremony. You looke sprightly friend.[2]

This play gives us yet another instance of the courtesy ob-served by inferiors to those above them. The first scene shows us the arrival of Contarino, the Duke's secretary, at the house of Charomonte, tutor to Cozimo's nephew and intended heir, Giovanni. The secretary has come to take Giovanni back to the court. As the noble youth enters Charomonte tells Contarino:

> Make your approaches boldly, you will finde
> A courteous entertainment.

Apparently the approach has included an attempt to kiss the young man's hand on bended knee; for Giovanni demurs:

> Pray you forbeare
> My hand, good Signior. 'Tis a ceremony
> Not due to me. 'Tis fit we should embrace
> With mutuall armes.

---

[1] Sig. C1ᵛ.   [2] Sig. C2ʳ.

To which Contarino replies:

> It is a favour Sir
> I grieve to be denide.

And Giovanni submits with modest grace:

> You shall o're-come.
> But 'tis your pleasure, not my pride that grants it.
> Nay pray you Guardian, and good Sir, put on:
> How ill it shewes to have that reverend head
> Be uncover'd to a boy?[1]

Ceremony of this kind is of the utmost importance in *King Lear*. It is the 'idol' which the King has worshipped, and which he continues to worship even after he has given up his throne. In the earlier parts of the play, particularly on his first entry, his stature is increased by the obsequiousness with which he is treated. His continued demands for the same elaborate courtesy lend colour, if not justice, to the complaints made by his two daughters against him; and when, by their command, the servants ignore him the shock must have been as sharp to Elizabethan sensibilities as that provided by the spectacle of the gentle, saintly Henry VI bending his anointed head submissively in surrender to his own misguided subjects.

It was apparently the detailed respect for rank and decorum that threw Macbeth's courtiers into confusion, so that all hung back dubiously, hesitating to pay their respects decently in correct sequence according to rank, until the Queen tells them not to stand upon the order of their going. The result is a hurried, undignified departure, in which the obvious absence of the proper forms demanded by the ordered pattern of the world provides a concrete example of chaos to parallel the spiritual disorder into which Scotland is disintegrating. And conversely, it is the orderly observance of ceremony towards the corrupt Claudius that adds an extra horror to the evil which has descended upon Denmark; for the Danes' joy in Hamlet's uncle not only helps to deceive an audience that knows nothing of the play, but continually reminds whoever knows the truth, of the

[1] Sig. B2v.

appalling reality, that whatever is rotten in the State is con-
triving successfully to maintain itself by blinding the normal
ability of ordinary people to distinguish good from evil. The
magnificent pomp of Claudius's departure in the second scene
of the play, with every sign of splendour, and none of mourning,
the ceremonious procession upon the long Elizabethan stage,
must have added weight to the Prince's incredulously bitter
'That it should come to this', when his father was but two months
dead.

As distinct from the upper classes, commoners were unpolished and inelegant, without the graces of mind and body
which were bestowed by a 'heroic education'. Their clothes
were not so splendid, even their weapons were clumsier. Where
the nobleman is adorned by a rapier, the citizen, and more
particularly the apprentice, carries a cudgel. Stephen's aspirations in *Every Man in his Humour* are expressed not only in his
vain attempts at the 'portly dignitie' of the noble, but also in his
'What, shall I walke with a cudgell like *Higgin-Bottom*? and
may haue a rapier, for money?' (II. iv).[1] Just as the nobility of the
superiors was shown in speech with facility of gesture, so the
commonness of commoners is expressed in the lack of these
accomplishments.

They who have *Hands* slow and ponderous [says Bulwer], and who
without any comelinesse beare and offer about their leaden *Hands*,
together with the arme, after a rusticall manner; so lifting it up sometimes, that they seeme to move a great lumpe of trembling flesh,
reaching their slow Right hand out timerously, as if they gave pro-
vender to an Elephant. Such are by this customary habit, discovered
to be Clownes, and men of a most unfaithfull memorie. Such men we
shall sometimes see so faint and idle in their discourse, that they stick
in the briers, and demurre in a grosse gesture of pronunciation; and
stricken as it were with astonishment, they seeme nailed to that ill
behaviour. This in old time, was called, *Agere suspensa manu*. For
that Clownes, and men not so well exercised in speaking, or such
whose unfaithfull memories faile them, while they are altogether

---

[1] B. Jonson, *Every Man in his Humour* (folio 1616), ed. Herford and Simpson, iii. 333.

ignorant of the matter, and are not certaine whither they shall be caried, or where they shall at length rest; they hang the *Hand*, and hold it as it were in suspense.[1]

The ordinary commoner was not 'exercised in speaking'; it was therefore as a result of their professionally acquired facility that the players drew upon themselves, until well into the eighteenth century, the complaint that they continued to act outside the theatre, to wear splendid clothes, to talk and swagger with the air of noblemen. Instead, their behaviour should have been in the 'familiar' style of the lower classes. This was the style of classical comedy, which, by definition, did not concern itself with the great, but only with those who did not behave in the grand style. The critics were justified in their objections to the mingling of grand and familiar. Commoners could be admitted to a minor part in tragedy, behaving 'decently' towards their superiors, without weakening the high style; on the contrary, the obsequious presence of the subject exaggerates the stature of the lord. But lowly personages occupy the foreground of comedy, which depends for its effect upon analysis of their petty weaknesses. To give full attention to their essentially ignoble spirit in tragedy would be to change the atmosphere of that kind of poem, turning it into something else. Conversely, to bring grand personages into comedy shatters the familiar style, unless the nobles are treated in such a way that they are no longer noble in bearing, and that to the renaissance mind would have been a contradiction in terms. That this sharp division between tragedy and comedy appears to us arbitrary and constricting is irrelevant: even those Elizabethans who were ignorant of the classical canon, and who enjoyed the mingling of the two in popular drama, would still be able to recognize that the existence of the separate 'kinds' corresponded to differences which in their own experience distinguished not merely the respective grades of society, but the whole attitude to life held by the nobleman from that which belonged to those beneath him. Whilst the popular dramatists mix tragic with comic elements,

---

[1] *Chiron.*, p. 117.

it is not their purpose to show noblemen familiarly. The nobles of popular drama, like those of classical tragedy, are not perfect; but, except in the case of specialized satire striking at individuals, not a class, their imperfections are not portrayed in such a style as to make the nobleman seem a commoner. Nor is the commoner shown as grand. According to Sir Richard Baker the popular stage observed decorum to the extent of restricting scurrilous speeches to equally scurrilous characters, who could be recognized by the audience as such:

Indeed, if they were put into the mouths of Princes, or Persons of gravity, there were just cause of dislike; but to be put into the mouths of scurrilous, and base persons, What hurt can they do? None to the Actours; for the *decorum* takes away their fault, and makes that faultless, which is *decent*, and less to the Spectatours: for how can *it infect them*, to imitate the scurrility, when they see it, comely for none, but scurrilous persons?[1]

Unless in disguise, a nobleman must not behave like a commoner, nor a good man like one who is bad. It was for this reason, I believe, that Shakespeare makes Hal denounce his drinking companions at the end of the second scene of *Henry IV, Part I*. As he speaks the soliloquy, 'I know you all', his 'action' changes to that of a prince. The seemingly low commoner is invested with majesty, and the Elizabethan audience knows that such scurrilous speeches as he may speak do not come from his soul, but are part of a disguise, as was confirmed by the evidence of history. Shakespeare could make certain that his contemporaries would not be thrown into moral confusion by the equivocal behaviour of the Prince.

The popular dramatists did not intend to abandon the decorum of personages which was preached by classicism; as a result, the words of Richard Edwardes apply to the popular stage as well as to the plays of the neo-classical school:

In comedies the greatest skill is this, rightly to touch
All things to the quick; and eke to frame each person so,

---

[1] Sir R. Baker, *Theatrum Triumphans* (1670), pp. 35–6.

That by his common talk you may his nature rightly know.
A roister ought not preach, that were too strange to hear;
But as from virtue he doth swerve, so ought his words appear.

Whether we are considering tragedy, or comedy, or tragi-comedy, or history, or any other of the kinds reeled off by Polonius, we must recognize that they were written by play-wrights, performed by actors, and witnessed by audiences who agreed with what Edwardes says about the manner in which the 'persons of the drama' ought to appear on the stage:

So correspondent to their kind their speeches ought to be.
Which speeches well-pronounc'd, with action lively framed
If this offend the lookers on, let Horace then be blamed,
Which hath our author taught at school, from whom he
    doth not swerve,
In all such kind of exercise decorum to observe.[1]

We have merely to read the popular dramatists to see that for the most part their characters are built upon a foundation provided by decorum. Giovanni, in *The Great Duke of Florence* (1636), is described by his tutor in such a way that we can see that this young nobleman's speeches corresponded to his kind, and were correctly pronounced (I. i):

                    my noble Charge,
By his sharp wit, and pregnant apprehension
Instructing those that teach him; making use
Not in a vulgar and pedantique forme
Of what's read to him, but 'tis streight digested
And truly made his owne. His grave discourse,
In one no more indebted unto yeares,
Amazes such as heare him; horsmanship
And skill to use his weapon are by practise
Familiar to him; as for Knowledge in
Musique, He needs it not, it being borne with him,
All that He speaks being with such grace deliver'd
That it makes perfit harmony.

This had been the impression made on all by Hamlet before first his grief for a dead father, and then his assumption of the

---

[1] *Damon and Pythias* (The Prologue), ed. J. S. Farmer (1906), pp. 3-4.

antic mood against a villainous uncle, led him to the point at which he asks whether it be 'nobler in the mind' to strike impetuously, or to continue biding his time in this most unheroic behaviour, a figure to whom even the tedious Polonius feels superior. An appreciation of the person imagined by Shakespeare as Ferdinand in *The Tempest* depends on our recognition of the grace with which he humiliates himself as Miranda's log-man. It is true that Prospero has power to force obedience: but the noble spirit, unless in love, would normally require all the weight of that power before submitting to such indignity. And even then submission would be accompanied by a resentment which is entirely absent in this case.

The unsuccessful attempts of commoners to behave like noblemen give rise frequently in Elizabethan drama to the kind of comedy exemplified in Molière's *Le Bourgeois Gentilhomme*. Simon Eyre in *The Shoemaker's Holiday* has no such aspirations: nevertheless the comedy, for Elizabethans, seems to have been provided not only by his honest insensitivity to rank, but also by his insistence upon making speeches, perpetrating, no doubt, most if not all of the 'solecisms' which are mentioned by Bulwer. Despite his wife's entreaties the worthy shoe-maker blunders inelegantly, if sincerely, on his way. On the other hand, it is precisely the fact that Tamburlaine is able to sway over to his side the army sent to subdue him that marks him as a monster, a prodigy. Not only has this untrained shepherd all the accomplishments of intellect of the carefully trained nobleman, but with these gifts go the regal presence of a warrior, the heroic stride, the flashing eye, the lofty brow of one who, though clad in shepherd's weeds, is going to conquer empires. The violent and deliberate breach of decorum helps to express the monstrous nature of this being, who was regarded by Marlowe's age, though possibly not by Marlowe, as literally a Scourge of God. When, however, Puntarvolo models his behaviour on that of noblemen in *Every Man out of His Humour*, Jonson has an opportunity to satirize the affectation of such courtiers as Osric. 'Study their carriage and behaviour', says Carlo. And in Act ii, Sc. ii,

when Puntarvolo goes through the ritual of addressing his own
wife, the text tells us what he does: 'I will step forward three
pases: of the which, I will barely retire one; and (after some
little flexure of the knee) with an erected grace salute her
(one, two, and three). Sweet lady, God saue you.' And
Carlo asks: 'Can any man walke more vpright then hee does?
Looke, looke; as if he went in a frame, or had a sute of wanescot
on: and the dogge watching him, lest he should leape out on't.'
Kitely, in *Every Man in His Humour* (Folio 1616), is afraid that
his companions will

> Make their loose comments, vpon euery word,
> Gesture, or looke, I vse.[1]

As well he may be; for the making of congees and legs needed
confidence and practised grace if it was to escape such comments
as Carlo's 'He makes congees to his wife in geometrical propor-
tions', as he witnesses another encounter between Puntarvolo
and his lady.

There appears to have been a conventional distinction between men of the court and men of the country, which showed
itself in such matters as bearing, and the paying of compliments.
Here again, the stage seems to be reflecting what was true of Elizabethan society: Vincent, the country gentleman in the dialogue
of *The English Courtier and the Country-gentleman* (1586), speaks
of himself as 'a plaine man, vtterly vnacquainted with disguising,
and superfluous ceremony'.[2] He objects that 'in the Towne it
seemeth . . . there is no meetinge of neighbours, without special
conuitation, no salutation without much respect & ceremony',[3]
and adds later that the city treatment of a gentleman was such
that 'if hee walke in the Cittie without seruants attending on
him, no man wil put off his cap or do him reuerence'.[4] It is clear
that the plain man might object to ceremony, but he still expected to be treated with reverence by inferiors. He says that
in the country this is given to gentlemen as such, whether
splendidly attended or not; 'if they hap to meet any such well

[1] Ed. Herford and Simpson, iii. 326.   [2] Ed. Hazlitt (1868), p. 11.
[3] Ibid., p. 31.   [4] Ibid., p. 43.

apparrelled person, in his worshipfull garmentes, or with a fayre
cheyne about his necke, the countrey lowtes (as you terme them)
can so much good manner, as to put off their hats, and if the
Gentleman be braue in deede, they will also doo him other
reuerence.'[1]

Ben Jonson's Downright is one of these persons 'of a rusticall
cut, I know not how, he doth not carry himself like a gentleman
of fashion'. But, as Welcome says, 'that's a grace peculiar to a
few'. Nevertheless, Downright lacks the sheer rustic boorish-
ness which earns Kent in *King Lear* a night in the stocks. The
rustic gentleman was still proud enough, if inelegant, in his
bearing not to be mistaken for a commoner. Vallentine, the
courtier in the dialogue from which I have just quoted, observes
of these unpolished gentry:

Touching their conuersation, you shall besides the rusticitie of their
houses and garments, finde them full of lofty lookes, barbarous behauiour, and vndecent dooinges. As for ensample, some one will laugh
when hee speaketh: an other will cough, before hee telles his tale:
and some will gape or yawne when hee giueth the hearinge. So as in
deede (vnlesse they be of better education) few doo know what
countenance to make among their equals, and among their betters
[are] vtterly to seeke. Also if they hap to dine at any table, either they
are sullenly silente, or els they fall into speeche of their owne
Auncestors, their owne landes, their owne wiues or children:
other subiect of talke yee shall seldome finde among these sortes of
countrey men.[2]

Servants as well as masters were expected to maintain a
standard of elegance at court. According to this dialogue, in
choosing servants 'wee regarde chiefly the comelinesse of the
person'. In *The Great Duke of Florence* (II. i) we are diverted
by the rustic awkwardness of Giovanni's servant, Calandrino,
arriving to pay his master's respects to Fiorinda. 'How the foole
stares', says Calaminta, the waiting-woman, as the new-comer
enters. Fiorinda agrees that he

> lookes as if he were
> Conning his neck-verse.

[1] Ed. Hazlitt (1868), p. 50.   [2] Ibid., p. 88.

Calandrino, hoping to prove perfect in his 'A.B.C. of Courtship', falters and stutters, consulting his notes, and after much confusion makes '*Antique curtesies*', carefully counting aloud the rhythm of his movements, 'One, two, three'.

We have to be careful to distinguish between the rustic, the plain, outspoken, but not inelegant man, and the boor of constitutional sullenness. Orlando in *As You Like It* has grounds for the grievances claimed traditionally by the younger brother who suffers from the law of primogeniture. He complains that Oliver 'keepes me rustically at home, or (to speak more properly) staies me heere at home vnkept . . . mines my gentility with my education' (I. i). The result is plain in his bearing. As Vallentine says in the Dialogue with the Country-gentleman, 'through rusticall company in childehoode, [they] doo get them selues as it were an habite in loughty lokes, clownish speech, and other vngentlemanly Iestures'.[1] And again: 'if you happen into the company of two Gentlemen, (though in wit and capacity alike) the one brought vp in the Countrey, the other in Court or Cittie, you shall euen at the first sight perceaue by their speeche, iesture, and behauiour, that their educations are diuerse.'[2] But it would not do to confuse Orlando with a boor like Morose. Orlando is rude, without polish, but he is noble. As Vallentine observes (and numerous Elizabethan writers agree with him): 'yet you must not thinke that these externall thinges, (I meane apparrell and iesture) bee the cheefest ornamentes for a Gentleman. For the inwarde vertues and perfections be in troth of most waight, and cheefly required.'[3] It is true that Orlando interrupts the Duke's meal in the forest with rude and violent threats,—he earns an urbane reprimand from Jaques, who reduces such heroics to lack of manners,—but left to himself he would develop into another Bussy d'Ambois, rather than a rustic clod. Bussy's lack of elegance misleads the Prince's Chamberlain into taking him for a broken-down soldier or a sort of jester-poet. But on a question of honour the new-comer to court is as

[1] Ibid., p. 69.   [2] Ibid., p. 85.
[3] Ibid., p. 86.

punctilious as any courtier, and far more formidable in his wrath. Orlando and Bussy are like Mercutio and Faulconbridge, except that the two latter are 'ornamented' by all the gloss of elegant nobility. But Morose is a low-bred, currish boor. His cold melancholy gives him the characteristics of a person whose fingers are all thumbs. He blunders, lashing out like an animal in pain, easily to be avoided but dangerous if he gets an adversary in a corner. His is the sullen stoical 'indolency' mentioned in *The Touchstone of Complexions*. Here, however, we find ourselves within the realm of renaissance physiology, an understanding of which is essential for the accurate reconstruction of any character in terms of Elizabethan acting.

Physiology and psychology, body and soul, are aspects of one another for the Elizabethan. A detailed treatment of this subject can hardly be given here; but it is necessary to stress the fact that *actio* merely showed through speech and gesture the state of the physiological secretions within the body, as well as what went on within the soul. 'Now as each body shall more especially participate any of these foure humors, the actions and gestures thereof, must needes be more precisely correspondent to that predominant quality.'[1] And whether simple or complicated, the physiological foundation of psychology determined ultimately how a person spoke and the manner of his 'action'. Moreover, Elizabethan actors were able to represent the various characteristics plainly enough for them to be perceived and understood by an audience.

Like physiology, the renaissance 'science' of physiognomy dealt with the significance of physical characteristics as the expression of variations of personality. It must always be a matter of some uncertainty how far the dramatist could rely on his audiences being able to see important details of physiognomy in the conditions of Elizabethan performance. Nevertheless, in the case of Richard III the actor was obviously able to represent the villainous physiognomy for which Crook-back Dick was

---

[1] J. P. Lomazzo, *The Artes of Curious Painting, Carving and Building*, tr. Haydocke (1598), sig. Aa vi^v (Bk. II, p. 12).

traditionally notorious. Certain details of 'action' treated by physiognomers, which could be represented successfully on the stage, are mentioned by Bulwer:

for as mens present passions and inclinations are brought by nature into act; so men following the vogue of nature, are wrought to a reiteration of that action, untill the *Hand* hath contracted a habit. The result of these Phisiognomers falls thus into a grand axiome of their art, that whosoever is (as by a personall propriety and actuall condition) customarily seen to use the gesture of any naturall affection; he is by habituall complexion very incident to that affection, exhibited by that gesture.[1]

Such signs are 'the gate, the turning of the eye, the finger on the head, and the wagging of the hand', and they 'shew a shamelesse wanton', as Ulysses notes of Cressida.

The physiognomical expression 'close-fisted' has become part of our common speech. I think it probable that a miser would be played with this habit of the hand, especially as 'to put forth the right hand spread, is the habit of bounty'. Bulwer adds, 'hence Phisiognomists say such who customarily use to hold the *Hand* extended out are of a liberall complexion of minde; arguing from this liberall property of the *Hand*'.[2] The performance of a role such as Faulconbridge, Mercutio, and Bussy d'Ambois would be affected by the traditional view of Socrates as a person in whom 'vehemencie of the *Hand*' was observed 'as a token of his violent nature and hot spirit'.[3] According to this view, moreover, 'such who have Hands too active in discourse, and use to beat the aire with an odious kinde of *Chiromachia*, bewray the cholerique transportation of their individuall natures, a habit of the *Hand* incident to young men'.[4]

Conversely, as we have already noticed, 'To use no Action at all in speaking, or a heavy and slow motion of the *Hand*, is the propertie of one stupid and sluggish'. The sluggishness, however, need not always be due to stupidity. A general slowness of movement with a calmness of disposition was characteristic of those whose complexion was phlegmatic; sluggishness, again,

[1] *Chirol.*, p. 73.　　　　　　[2] Ibid., pp. 61–2.
[3] *Chiron.*, p. 112.　　　　　　[4] Ibid., p. 111.

might be caused by melancholy, whether temperamental or transitory. This inability to move quickly, together with the accompanying habit of mind, constitutes what is called 'Tarditie' in the 1598 translation of Lomazzo's *The Arte of Curious Painting*.

Tarditie makes a man slow and heavie in all his actions: whose proper gesture is to stande still, mooving the armes, and the rest of his body slowly, not much mooving, or spreading the legges, which when they are once fixed in a place, be not easily altered; as in men that forget themselues, porters, and clownes. . . . And after this manner shal you shew old folkes, but especially grosse and country people.[1]

A clown, who is not necessarily a funny man, but certainly without grace, might well be shown as one of 'such men who sit crowching in the world with their arms a-crosse, their mouths gaping, and their feet in one shooe'.[2] A gesture fit for these is described by Bulwer as *Otio indulgeo*: 'to fold the Hands, is a gesture of *idlenesse*, an expression often seene in the *Hands* of *lazy* Lubbers amus'd with *sloath*, who keepe their *dull Hands* so knit together, to *maintain a drowsie league with sleepe*'.[3] This was the gesture with which Hamlet may well have said ruefully that he, being John-a-dreams, 'can say nothing' (II. ii).

The teachings of Physiognomers concerning the significance of the left hand correspond to the cautions against its use in rhetorical action given by writers like Bulwer. There are cases, however, when the left hand alone could be used on the stage. Bulwer has collected a great deal of evidence which shows that as far back as classical antiquity, as well as in his own day, this hand was regarded as peculiarly appropriate to the habits of a thief. Gestus LXIII in *Chirologia*, called 'Furacitatem Noto' (marked Y in Fig. 3), says as follows:

To put forth the left Hand as it were by stealth, is their significant endeavour who have *an intent unseene to purloine and convey away something*. From which fellonious action the Adage is derived, *Vtitur manu sinistra*, which translated, in the proverbiall sense is tooke up against cheates, and pilfering fellowes, who by a *theevish sleight of*

---

[1] Op. cit., sig. Cc ij^r. (Bk. II, p. 27.) [2] *Chirol.*, p. 37.
[3] Ibid., pp. 35–6.

Hand, and slie way of robbery, can bereave one of a thing unperceived; for such *Mercurialists* who addresse themselves to filch, and lurching closely assay *under-Hand* to steale a thing *Hand-smooth* away, doe in the cursed *Handicraft* of theft, out of a kinde of cunning choice imploy the left hand. . . . A *Hand* which if it once grow dexterious by habituall theeving, will not be left; for if it once affect to keep it selfe in ure, it turnes to an incurable felon. [Theft was punished by a brand on the left thumb in the first offence.] And if it may be lawful to divine of the legality of this law-checke, I should thinke that there lyes some concealed symboll in the device, and that the estates assembled had regard to the fellonious procacity and craft of this guilefull *Hand*, which is prone by a slie insinuation with more subtile secrecie to present it selfe to any sinister intention, & doth no sooner move to such actions, but every finger proves a limetwig.

As a result the ancient Egyptians 'figured furacity or theft by a light fingured left hand put forth as it were by stealth'. The following are the teachings of the ancients on this subject:

First, it is the noted property of the left hand to be coverd, and to keep as it were a recluse in the bosome, or to be carried wrapped up in a cloake, lurking closely and lying as it were in ambuscado to entrap, and by a crafty fetch imperceptibely to make a prize of all that comes to *Hand* . . . this hand being more idle, for idlenesse is a maine cause of theft, it is consequently more prone to this manuall transgression. This light-fingered hand being called by *Isidor*, *Læva quod aptior sit ad levandum*, to wit, to beguile, elude, lessen and diminish anothers goods. And *Theocritus* following herein the opinion of antiquity, having noted the particular quality and behaviour of this hand, and the private vice to which it is propense, concludes from the pitchy temper thereof, that the left hand signifies the captivity of unlawfull desire and rapacity; so that it hath for this cause been consecrated to *Laverna* the goddesse of theeves, as being by reason of its wily genius more fit and convenient for cousenage and clandestine theevery; for being commonly hid and involved in the bosome of a gown or cloake and waiting in obscurity, it comes to passe for the most part (men suspecting no such thing) that doing nothing and devoted to rest, yet being at liberty and ready to handle, it will be doing, and somewhat of other mens suffers for it, while this purloining hand thinkes it selfe the proprietary of anothers goods.[1]

[1] *Chirol.*, pp. 133-6.

Among the quotations from past literature illustrating the same attitude to the left hand comes an account of how the bawd in *Persa* asks to see the hand of Paeginum, but he, 'like a crafty wag had put forth his *Right Hand*; she replied to him *ubi illa altera furtifica læva*, where is that other close and cunning pilferer the left hand'. Shakespeare's Autolycus was 'littered under Mercury'; thus he like other 'Mercurialists' would use the left hand. The probability that this was the 'snapper up of unconsidered trifles' is strengthened by Bulwer's reference to the classical Autolycus immediately after the quotation from the Roman comedy. Autolycus was expert, he tells us, 'in the slie feats of this hand, of whom *Martial*,

> *Non erat Autolici tam piceata manus.*'[1]

This is not conclusive, but shows that as late as 1644 the name was associated with the use of the left hand, whose 'every finger . . . a limetwig' would have proved formidable weapons for the gay and crafty figure in *The Winter's Tale*.

If we are entitled to regard the fingers of the left hand as 'pickers and stealers', the meaning of Hamlet's cryptic remark to Rosencrantz at once becomes clear (III. ii). His former friend reproaches the Prince: 'My Lord, you once did loue me.' And as Hamlet gives the reply he raises the left hand as though swearing an oath, but widdershins. It was normal to raise the right hand when swearing an oath. According to Bulwer, 'The Angels also when they sweare doe it not without this manuall asseveration'. To raise both hands was

a *double oath* . . . . Such an *asseveration* of gesture I lately observed in some at the publique taking of the last Nationall Covenant, who as I conceived rather out of a zealous earnestnesse to ingage themselves in the Cause, then out of any affectation or privity to this double formality of a Vow, tooke the Covenant with both their Hands held up.[2]

Another symbol, but one which is closely tied to physiognomy, is 'to hold the fingers inserted between each other a-crosse,' (marked K in Fig. 2). This is 'their *sluggish* expression who are

---

[1] *Chirol.*, p. 136.   [2] Ibid., pp. 51–2.

fallen into a *melancholy muse*'.[1] He tells us that according to Pliny the presence of a bystander in this posture has an adverse effect upon any undertaking which may happen to be under consideration at the time. This gesture of the fingers would therefore suit Hamlet's remark that enterprises

> With this regard their Currants turne away,
> And loose the name of Action.

Innocentiam ostendo is Bulwer's label for a gesture of which he says, 'to imitate the posture of washing the Hands by rubbing the back of one in the hollow of the other with a kind of deter-sive motion, is a gesture sometimes used by those who would *professe their innocency*, and declare *they have no Hand in that foule businesse, not so much as by their manuall assent*; as it were by assuring by that gesture, that *they will keepe their Hands un-defiled*, and *would wash their Hands of it: nor have any thing to doe therein*' (marked L in Fig. 2).[2] We are accustomed to the use of this symbol by Pilate, and by Lady Macbeth in the sleep-walking scene. Mrs. Siddons was justified in her breach with eighteenth-century tradition when she set down the candle and returned to at least one detail of Elizabethan stage business as the Doctor says, 'It is an accustom'd action with her, to seeme thus washing her hands' (v. i). There is also a strong possibility that this gesture was used by the mutes as Richard is led past them to captivity. They shift uneasily, and try to deny their guilt as the deposed king says with scorn (IV. i):

> Though some of you, with *Pilate*, wash your hands,
> Shewing an outward pittie: yet you *Pilates*
> Haue here deliuer'd me to my sowre Crosse,
> And Water cannot wash away your sinne.

A consideration of character in the light of rhetorical acting involves attention to the minutiae of physiology, psychology, and physiognomy. Age, rank, and occupation must be taken into account as well as all the details of bearing and behaviour which are set forth in those sciences. Quite a number of modern prob-lems disappear when we remember that, unless given any reason

---

[1] Ibid., pp. 38–9.   [2] Ibid., p. 40.

to think otherwise, the Elizabethan audience accepted the actor's words as expressing the character's thoughts. And the actor, instead of asking himself what the character was thinking when uttering these words, concentrated on giving the correct 'action', on the correct use of voice and gesture to express the meaning and emotion in the words themselves. The audience was interested in his outside as an expression of the imaginary character's inside. From this point of view it is possible to detect three kinds of persons imagined by the writers of Elizabethan drama. First come those people whose 'outer show' is a true indication of the reality within. These are people who, whether honest or criminal, show their true selves to their fellow men; it is possible to calculate the reactions of such people and having observed their faults to beware of them. Elizabethan psychology taught that it was natural to show emotions, to allow what was within to be seen from without; frankness in this sense was valued as much in the early seventeenth century as in the novels of Jane Austen.

The second kind of character in Elizabethan drama is not so healthy; he betrays no emotion; he is the stoic, whose 'indolency' was decried by Lemnius and Bulwer. A man who shows no reaction is an incalculable force; and to the Elizabethans, even ignoring the philosophy of Machiavelli, a person to be regarded with suspicion. Massinger's Cozimo in *The Great Duke of Florence* becomes a deeply menacing figure as soon as he begins to hide his thoughts and feelings from his courtiers, so that they are unable to calculate his intentions and forecast his actions.

But the third kind of person is the most dangerous of all. Instead of concealing his personality under an impassive appearance which expresses nothing, he appears superficially exactly the opposite of his true self. No better example can be found than that of Claudius. His seeming is the opposite of his being; but so plausible is he that it takes half a play to demonstrate to the audience, and the whole play to show his court of Denmark, that beneath his smile there lurks a villain.

The difficulties in the way of seeing into another's heart are often at the basis of tragedy, particularly in those of Shakespeare. Othello mistakes both Iago and Desdemona, Gloster both Edgar and Edmund; Lear is blind to Goneril and Regan as well as to the reality inside Cordelia. Here, we have penetrated to one of the fundamental truths of which the Elizabethan was sure to be conscious, as soon as he paused to consider seriously the implications of a story dealing with the consequences of a serious mistake. Man, unlike God, cannot see into the heart; as a result, not only is appearance mistaken for reality, but frequently the sound testimony of outer show is rejected when it truthfully expresses the reality within. With Elizabethan acting an audience could hardly fail to perceive the existence of such possibilities, and their relation to the story represented on the stage. No specialized intellectual training is needed to appreciate the situation in which Iago, who has exulted in evil before our eyes, exchanges the 'action' of a soul given over to Satan for the seeming appearance of one whose honesty is his ruling principle. The seeming honesty is so like what it imitates that only those who have seen the devil within can know, or even suspect, that the show without tells a lie. Aaron, in *Titus Andronicus*, is one whose black exterior fits the black soul within; but the white devil, the hypocrite,[1] is white outside whilst no less black than the Moor within. As a result we find the term 'White Devil' used as an alternative to 'hypocrite', and the title of Webster's play indicated to his contemporaries the nature of Vittoria, and his awareness of it.

Lear's mistake, blinded as he is by pride, is to ignore the true meaning of Cordelia's outer show. I have observed elsewhere[2] that she was probably played at the Globe as one whose temperament did not lend itself to that felicitous employment of speech

---

[1] According to Thomas Adams, *The White Devil, or The Hypocrite Uncased* (1613), Luther named Judas 'the *white Deuill*', because 'a Deuill hee was, blacke within and full of rancour, but white without and skinned ouer with hypocrisie' (p. 1). This sermon was printed five times between 1613 and 1629.

[2] *Elizabethan Acting*, an introductory essay to Shakespeare's *Plays* awaiting publication by Winchester Publications Ltd.

and gesture which the Elizabethans expected of an uninhibited nobleman or noblewoman on the stage. Briefly, it seems from the text that Cordelia's action was 'ponderous', with enough of the marks of a 'tardy' person to enable the audience to appreciate that her very nature will not allow her to reply with the unrestrained warmth which alone will satisfy her father. And yet it is no less clear that her love is in truth 'more ponderous than' her tongue. When cold logic has failed and she is disinherited the audience knows that what her father wants is monstrous. And in case the Elizabethans were not certain of Cordelia, as the King, her father, leaves, they were reassured by the King, to be her husband, that her bearing and her apparent coldness are the result of nothing more than a tardiness 'in nature'. Persons of a phlegmatic complexion, with a sweetness of nature, are described as behaving like Cordelia in renaissance works on psychology and physiology. The King of France is the only king present on the stage apart from Lear; only the man who is going to marry Cordelia is equal in dignity to her father; as a result, when this noble personage condescends to her in her humiliation, it is plain to the audience that she may have been right and Lear wrong when she said: 'So young my Lord, and true.' Cordelia's bearing shows patience, not stoicism; she has resiliency, not unbending stiffness. When she returns with her French army she can find it in her to treat her father courteously and gently; indeed, her 'action' now expresses her insistence on the validity of natural bonds, even more powerfully in her unbending than when it had won for her the rebuke 'So young and so untender'. The beginning of the play shows natural ties being broken, its end shows them knitting together again, reaffirming harmony, even as Lear wakes to 'consent' of music after the discordances of pride and madness.

Elizabethan acting probably lent itself to parts involving imposture and disguise. To assume the salient features of another's 'action' would not be too difficult; and in the case of disguise, change of clothes would be accompanied by change of voice and bearing complete enough to suggest a new personality. A

disguise which seems to have been very effective is the adoption
of a lower rank. In *King Lear* this preserves Edgar and Kent;
in *The Revenger's Tragedy* (I. iii) it is responsible for a passage of
dialogue which enables us to visualize the scene on the Elizabethan stage. Vindice enters with the question, 'am I farre inough
from my selfe', and receiving the assurance,

> As if another man had beene sent whole
> Into the world,

invokes 'Impudence' so boldly that his brother warns him 'settle
your lookes', as Lusurioso approaches. Vindice's new role is that
of a bluff, impudent henchman, another Bosola. He responds to
Lusurioso's 'be bould with vs, thy hand' by seizing that personage's hand, saying:

> With all my heart, yfaith how dost sweete Musk-cat
> When shall we lie togither?

The offensive and familiar vigour with which Vindice works
Lusurioso's arm is reflected in the remark:

> Wondrous knaue!
> Gather him into bouldnesse, Sfoote, the slaue's
> Already as familiar as an Ague,
> And shakes me at his pleasure.

And then, with an assumption of authority and hauteur:

> Friend, I can
> Forget my selfe in priuate; but else where,
> I pray do you remember me.

Vindice has not merely disguised himself; he has assumed a
personality which is superficially entirely the opposite of that
belonging to the malcontent, on whom the play opened, 'sighing
ore deaths vizard'.

When Shakespeare's *Timon of Athens* is considered in the light
of Elizabethan acting, and of the tradition respecting the relation
of spirit to outer show, the play can be seen as illustrating a clear
pattern of thought. Timon is the supreme sham; there is nothing

inside his shell, no personality at all; that is why he can be called *Misanthropos*. At the beginning of the play he receives all the adulation of a monarch, and seems liberal; but as the flattery of his sycophants is shown to be false, so his seeming liberality reveals the prodigal whose pride has brought his downfall. If we measure the seemingly magnificent Timon against the really noble Alcibiades, we can see who lacks greateartedness. Alcibiades pleads for his friend, and takes the second chance which Fortune offers; Timon, in misfortune, finds no consolation. Lear was comforted by one faithful follower, but the existence of his honest steward in no way mitigates Timon's ignoble grovelling. Measure Timon against Apemantus and we see who has and who has not deliberately weighed the things of the world and dispassionately found them valueless. Where Apemantus has done this and ordered his life accordingly, Timon, soured by miseries of his own making, has spirit left only to deride what he once valued, not because he can distinguish between the gold and the dross, but because now there is nothing left but the hope that all is dross to give bite to the impotent acid of his misery. Unlike Alcibiades, Timon has not the spirit to profit by experience, and take the second chance that he is offered.

The play opens with what is virtually a dumbshow of adulation, with all Athens thronging Timon's lobbies, whilst the Poet and Painter act as presenters, and suggest what possibilities might develop in the course of the action (I. i). Whereas the Poet declares that Timon's fortune,

> Vpon his good and gracious Nature hanging,
> Subdues and properties to his loue and tendance
> All sorts of hearts,

including Apemantus, the Painter says nothing more than the curt, non-committal 'I saw them speake together'. And when, a few moments later, we see Timon greeted by Apemantus, it is in a manner which belies the Poet's enthusiasm. 'Till I be gentle, stay thou for thy good-morrow', says the Philosopher, and a few lines further on we find Timon remonstrating, 'Thou art proud

Apemantus', to get the reply, 'Of nothing so much, as that I am not like *Timon*'.

The first scene with the Poet and the Painter sounds a warning amidst the bustle and splendour of Timon's ante-rooms. We are told that Fortune has beckoned him to her, and we know that a time must soon come when she will spurn him away again. And the Painter tells his companion (I. i):

> Yet you do well,
> To shew Lord *Timon* that mean eyes haue seene
> The foot aboue the head.

The play now proceeds to show us whether Timon is in actual fact the foot above the head. Our next warning comes when he accepts the 'peece of Painting' from the Painter.

> The Painting is almost the Naturall man,

says Timon,

> For since Dishonor Traffickes with mans Nature,
> He is but out-side: These Pensil'd Figures are
> Euen such as they giue out.

The first line has two meanings, that the painting looks almost like the model, and that it resembles the innocence of unfallen man. The second meaning is now elaborated, and the point is stressed that, whereas since the Fall man has nothing within and everything without, the soul of a painting is in its outside. The appearance truly expresses the spirit. Shakespeare returns to this point in the interview with Apemantus to which I have just called attention. Asked how he likes the picture, the Philosopher replies:

> The best, for the innocence.

The contrast between appearance and reality would never be absent from the mind of the audience who saw this play acted in the Elizabethan manner. An actor who had been trained in this style, and who knew how to pronounce the literary text, would automatically create upon the stage the kind of person imagined by the dramatist at any particular moment. It is dangerous to generalize about a matter so complicated as the representation of the personages of Elizabethan drama: nevertheless, no harm and much good can be done if instead of trying to deduce what might be in the mind of an imaginary character as he expresses himself, we try to imagine the appearance of an Elizabethan actor when pronouncing those same words. Then we may be able to gauge accurately the kind of impression made upon the audiences for whom the play was written; and when every scene in a play has been treated in this manner it often happens that 'problems of characterization' have completely disappeared.

VI

THE GROUNDS OF CRITICISM IN
ELIZABETHAN DRAMA

WHAT are the grounds of criticism in Elizabethan drama? This is a question which has been asked repeatedly during the twentieth century by critics no longer satisfied with the judgements pronounced by the naturalists. Once, it was assumed[1] that drama was the kind of art most admirably suited to the realistic imitation of what William Archer called 'the audible and visible surfaces of life'. It was stated that only when the playwright contrived to imitate these surfaces realistically was he writing drama as it ought to be written. The naturalistic conception of drama was first propounded with logical consistency by Castelvetro in his *Poetica d'Aristotele* in 1570. Here he stated that the purpose of all poetry is the imitation of life: and that therefore the poet's method must be verisimilitude. Examining non-dramatic poetry —in particular the epic—Castelvetro insists that the poet's medium is inadequate. An imitation of life, in this critic's view, involves a rendering of the 'things and words' in the poem as they are to be found in the original. By 'things and words', he means the people in the story and their actions, the clothes they wear, the houses they live in, the horses they ride, the weapons they wield, and in addition the words which they speak and the thoughts they think. The writer of epic can imitate with verisimilitude the words and thoughts of real life: but the 'things' cannot be realistically imitated by means of words. In this respect, therefore, the epic poet is bound to fail. But the dramatic poet not only uses 'words' for his imitation; he has at his disposal a theatre and actors. Like the epic writer, the dramatist can imitate 'words' by means of words, but in addition he has

---

[1] *Poetica d'Aristotele* (1570), p. 16; *vide* H. B. Charlton, *Castelvetro's Theory of Poetry* (1913), p. 84.

'things' where in epic 'words' still have to be used. For the next three hundred years dramatic theory and practice developed in Europe in accordance with this conception of the art. Once the medium of drama was considered to be a mixture of words and things, there followed naturally the insistence that words should be restricted in a play to the imitation of words which would be spoken in real life; and gradually the demand for verisimilitude led to the point at which soliloquy was abandoned, whilst dialogue must be fashioned in such a way as to present a realistic imitation of what the speakers might be expected to say in a similar situation in real life. The logical result of thinking about drama, and of writing it in this manner, is the kind of dialogue which we find in the naturalistic theatre of the late nineteenth century, where in a play like *Die Familie Selicke* every attempt is made to reproduce the pauses, circumlocutions—and where suitable the stammering and stuttering—to be found in the by no means coherent speech of everyday life.

Critics like William Archer recognized the part played by the poetic quality of renaissance drama; but with the results—the naturalists would have said achievements—of naturalism in mind they insisted that this quality was not necessary to a play. In their view poetry, however magnificent in itself, was liable to divert the author from his main purpose of presenting a realistic imitation of surfaces such as we see and hear in everyday life. They looked on Elizabethan drama as representing a phase in the development of naturalistic drama, a phase in which it is possible to demonstrate that authors of dramatic talent in the modern sense have neglected to rid themselves of naïveties of technique, and inconsistencies of plot and character, because they can rely on the power of language to hide these blemishes from a complaisant audience. A classic example of criticism deriving from this attitude is to be found in the comment of an editor of *Macbeth* upon what he regards as 'the magnificently irrelevant soliloquies of the great protagonist himself'.[1]

In his attack upon the habit of attempting to judge Shake-

[1] *Macbeth*, ed. H. Cunningham (1913), p. xxii.

speare by naturalistic standards of criticism, Professor L. C. Knights decided: 'There is something wrong with a conception of "the dramatic" which leads a critic to speak of Macbeth's final soliloquies as irrelevant, even though magnificent.'[1] It is true that the naturalistic conception of drama must inevitably lead us astray in evaluating the work of the Elizabethans. Nevertheless, we are not justified in declaring that 'there is something wrong' with that conception in itself: it has been responsible, it is true, for the virtual disappearance of poetic drama; but it has also been responsible for the appearance of a new class of great prose dramas, which could otherwise never have been written. We should recognize in our desire to do justice to the Elizabethans that there is no need to do injustice to the naturalists. Their conception of drama is valid, but only when applied to plays written in accordance with it: and their criteria must not be applied to the Elizabethans. Unfortunately, however, this is exactly what we do; we often judge Shakespeare and his contemporaries in accordance with the naturalistic conception of drama, without intending to do so, and because we have not been able to arrive at a clear understanding of the principles governing the Elizabethans in their art.

What, then, it may be asked, is the right conception of drama which will prevent our misunderstanding the essentials of the Elizabethan art? It is not enough to insist that poetry is relevant; for Mr. Eliot, who always recognized the part it played, still found the Elizabethans inconsistent in the use of what are to-day called conventions. Despite Miss Bradbrook's insistence[2] on the need to ignore the standards which we apply to other drama, and despite also Mr. Bethell's explanation[3] of the Elizabethan ability to ignore the apparent inconsistencies which, however disconcerting to the modern mind, are actually irrelevant, the normal view is still that which we find in Mr. Eliot's *Four Elizabethan Dramatists*. Writing in answer to Archer as long ago

---

[1] *How Many Children had Lady Macbeth?* (1933), p. 34, note 1.
[2] *Themes and Conventions of Elizabethan Tragedy* (1935), p. 4.
[3] *Shakespeare and the Popular Dramatic Tradition* (1944).

as 1924, he declared: 'What is fundamentally objectionable is that in Elizabethan drama there has been no firm principle of what is to be postulated as a convention and what is not.'[1]

Time after time in our reading of the Elizabethans, and in our attempts to perform them, it appears at first sight as if Mr. Eliot's remark is justified. There seems no consistency, for instance, in Shakespeare's use of conventions in a famous scene in *The Third Part of Henry VI* (II. v). The whirl of battle has left an empty stage for the entrance of Henry, unattended, to tell us of 'the equall poise of this fell Warre'. Longing for death, 'For what is in this world, but Greefe and Woe', the King lets his thoughts dwell upon the sweet security of a pastoral life, concluding that its ordered calm is preferable to the pomp and splendour of a monarch, 'When Care, Mistrust, and Treason waits on him'. The stage direction reads '*Alarum*'; and at one door enters the burdened figure of '*a Sonne that hath kill'd his Father*'. As he greedily prepares to pillage the body of his victim, the Son discovers that he has unwittingly slain his Father, and joy in the slaughter changes to an outburst of wild remorse. As Henry breaks into a lament upon this 'pitteous spectacle' a second burdened figure comes in at another door. This time it is '*a Father that hath kill'd his Sonne*'. And again the victor makes a terrible discovery. As his two subjects exclaim their horror at a monstrous crime, committed in blind ignorance, Henry cries out in 'greefe, more thē common greefe'. His sense of personal inadequacy is such that, as they go out, miserably burdened, all their joy in killing gone, he breaks into apostrophe:

> Sad-hearted-men, much ouergone with Care;
> Heere sits a King, more wofull then you are.

Unfortunately, as soon as we begin to imagine this scene in terms of the theatre, a number of difficulties present themselves to the modern mind. We wonder how it is possible for human beings to represent the speakers on the stage. Where are they to stand, in what directions are they to turn, what are they to do with their hands whilst declaiming long speeches, to whom shall

[1] *Selected Essays, 1917–32* (1932), p. 115.

they address themselves, and what shall each do whilst the others are speaking? We usually try to answer questions such as these by asking ourselves another question: how would real men behave if they were involved in the situation which we see in the drama? And as a result we then try to interpret every speech as representing something which can take place in the world in which plays are imagined and performed, instead of in the mind of the author who imagined the play. In the real world human beings either speak their thoughts to themselves in monologue, or communicate them to others in dialogue. In so far as silent thoughts are silent in real life, the argument runs, they should not be represented unrealistically by words spoken aloud on the stage; instead, plays ought to be written with such skill that only the visible and audible surfaces of life need to be imitated in the expression of the writer's purpose. If monologue is to be used, it must be limited to that kind which represents the thoughts which might really be spoken aloud.

The most convenient terminology for distinguishing between the two kinds of monologue just mentioned is that used by M. L. Arnold. The speech which represents words spoken aloud he calls 'verbal soliloquy', whilst referring to the representation of silent thoughts as 'mental soliloquy'.[1] But Elizabethan drama is universally admitted to employ yet another kind of monologue in which the 'person of the drama' does something which is not done in real life, and which obliges the performer in the theatre to address his words to his audience. A speech of this kind, known as 'direct address', is usually regarded as a vestige of the primitive technique which had not disengaged itself from the methods of non-dramatic poetry. Once we have identified every speech in a scene as either dialogue or one of the three kinds of monologue we can proceed to perform the lines, or to imagine their performance when reading, in the following manner. Dialogue is addressed to one or more of the persons of the drama. 'Mental soliloquy' is not addressed to anyone else, and whoever is present with the speaker makes no sign of having

[1] M. L. Arnold, *The Soliloquies of Shakespeare* (1911), p. 20.

heard the speech. 'Verbal soliloquy' is not addressed to anybody, but can be heard by whoever is present. 'Direct address' is spoken to the audience. With this rough and ready division in mind, let us return to the scene in *Henry VI, Part III*, and try to pass a fair and unbiased judgement on the skill or clumsiness with which the dramatist has done his work.

Henry's first speech does not offer any obvious difficulty. We can accept it as 'mental soliloquy', but with the reservation that it is too formal and stiff in its style and rhythm to carry conviction as representing the way in which the king could really have been thinking to himself at a moment like this. The theme is developed too logically, with too much attention to figures of words, and with no suggestion of spontaneity, particularly in so far as the last section is preceded by the formula 'And to conclude'. This might suit a school oration, but is out of place in the urgency of the moment in which Henry is speaking. Now let us look at the Son's first speech: 'Ill blows the wind that profits nobody.' It cannot be 'mental soliloquy' as the words are heard by the king, and it is hardly likely to be dialogue, as there is no certainty that at any moment in the scene either of his subjects is aware of his presence. We might be justified, therefore, in assuming that the son's words as he enters are 'verbal soliloquy'; and again the comment might be added that no man is likely to cry his grief aloud in this way at such a moment. With the entrance of the third speaker the problem becomes even more complicated. In so far as Henry can hear their speeches, these cannot represent 'mental soliloquy'; but his speeches do not seem to be spoken aloud, as they are not heard by his subjects. Again, in so far as he can hear them, we should expect them to hear one another. At one moment words spoken aloud on the stage represent words spoken aloud in real life; at another, the words spoken aloud in the play seem intended to be interpreted as what would be silent thought in real life. It would obviously be ridiculous to continue analysing the scene in this manner before coming to a decision as to its dramatic merit. Nevertheless, we see that Mr. Eliot had grounds for his assertion that the Elizabethans are inconsistent in the use of their own conventions. And the charge has even greater weight when we pause to remember that some, or perhaps all, of the speeches here might be 'direct address'. How are we to distinguish the one from the other?

Do we need to distinguish one from the other? Is it essential for us to recognize a speech in an Elizabethan play as representing dialogue or a particular kind of monologue before we can respond to the author's use of his medium so that we imagine his play in his terms? When Shakespeare imagined this scene he did not concern himself with what might actually have happened if the king had encountered his subjects in this deserted part of the battle-field. Instead there is a pause in the development of what has been known later as 'the intrigue': we are not presented with a new incident in the story, but with a new glimpse at what we have already seen taking place in England—civil war. And now the poet's point of view is one which shows us all the more horrible implications of the struggle, making us imagine it with his sensibility. To convey the meaning of the horrors to us, to make us take in at one glance the essence of the situation as it strikes him, the dramatist has expressed himself by means of symbols; his technique, in its deliberate lack of realism, enables him to achieve his purpose economically, yet with force. He seems to have been aware of Henry at this moment, above all, as a weak king, whose individual piety ensures rather than prevents his being engulfed in the disintegration of the social structure, an inevitable consequence of the Lancastrian usurpation of the English throne. Shakespeare makes us understand why writers like Thomas Gainsford thought of civil war as, literally, 'a worke of the diuell'.[1] We are induced to imagine the violent cunning of a 'cursed spite' which is making of England a little hell, a realm where, as in Satan's vaster empire, all is, again in the words of Thomas Gainsford, 'full of confusions, horrours, and vtter disorders'.[2] First, however, we are made to yearn with

---

[1] T. Gainsford, *The Rich Cabinet* (1616), sig. L2ᵛ.
[2] Ibid., sig. P3ʳ.

Henry for the healthy order of pastoral routine. There is no need to deplore that at the beginning of this scene the King's speech is 'unnatural' in the studied concentration of its thought and language. If we forget 'nature' and realism we can allow the deliberate repetition of sounds and phrases, with measured intervals of time, to create an ordered picture of a life in which natural processes run their steady uninterrupted course. The reiteration of the phrases 'How many days', and 'So many hours' helps to make us feel the serenity of the days and years imagined by the king, stretching in prospect to the peaceful ending of a grave where one can look back on

> Minutes, Houres, Dayes, Monthes, and Yeares,
> Past ouer to the end they were created.

Shakespeare's contemporaries shared his attitude to order: they too could exult in the thought of its naturalness and holiness. The Elizabethan common reader was accustomed to such passages as the following, in Gainsford's *The Rich Cabinet*:

Order framed the world, setled the heauens, proportioned the motions of the Sunne, Moone and Starres in their seasons; embelished the earth with infinite varieties of flowers and fruits in their seasonable times; limited the seas with banks and bounds; and set an orderly course in all creatures.[1]

But Shakespeare allows us to enjoy the harmony of this concept only long enough to make us rue the full bitterness of its loss. The king comes to his despondent conclusion, and the calm is shattered, as a Son and a Father stand before us stained with murder, self-condemned. Hell has burst its bounds: England has become a chaos of floundering broken ties. As the king stands by, ignored and useless, raising his voice to strengthen the lamentations of his horrified subjects, there is no need for reader or audience to ask which speeches are monologue or dialogue, which represent silent thoughts or words spoken audibly. Our response must be to language 'animated with action'.

[1] Op. cit., sig. P3^r.

Shakespeare was writing at a time when kings were normally regarded as 'Gods on earth', as well as the heads of the body politic and the fathers of their subjects. He could therefore use the motif of a broken link between Father and Son to relate family chaos to a more central disorder, involving not merely the ties between subjects and their king, but the very bonds which link all men—kings, nobles, or commoners—to their God. The grief of the slayers is personal in its intensity and manner of expression, but it none the less symbolizes the grief of every Englishman. And the bitterness of the grief emphasizes rather than obscures the reality of a guilt which is likewise both personal and common to all the inhabitants of the land. It is true that the sin was committed in ignorance: but the poet is insisting that civil war is essentially an ignoring of natural relationships. To kill your countryman is a crime of the same kind as to kill your own relations.

But the monstrousness of this conflict is not limited to strife between natural equals: as in *Lear*, Shakespeare shows us the horror of the foot against the head, and the head against the foot. Here we can recognize a symbolic portrayal of the Devil's work. The scene hardly resembles the visible and audible surfaces of life as the three speakers declaim in linked speeches. Instead, the author induces us to imagine the horrid realities of civil war in his terms, preparing us for the descent farther into chaos in that harrowing moment when Henry is to yield meekly to the challenge of the two commoners who no longer acknowledge his rights to their obedience. The king's submission to the game-keepers is the kind of offence against order which can be symbolized by the figure of a Father slain by his own Son: moreover, Henry is himself acquiescing in a deed which will bring misery to his people, to whom he stands now as a Father working evil against his own children.

If we are to criticize the scene in which Shakespeare uses symbols to depict what is spiritually wrong with England, surely there is no need to test each utterance as a representation, realistic or unrealistic, of what might have happened in an actual

battle. There is no need to distinguish dialogue from monologue, 'mental' from 'verbal soliloquy', or all three from 'direct
address'. The ability to recognize these categories of dramatic
speech does not contribute to our response. But we have to
recognize the symbols and their meaning. And, therefore, our
criticism should be directed towards the manner in which the
poet has organized them so that the relationship of the ideas
which they express towards the theme of his play strikes us
clearly and forcibly. The author is to be judged according to the
skill with which he has developed his thought in the scene itself:
every speech can be tested as contributing to or detracting from
the coherence of the exposition, just as the scene itself is to be
regarded in the same manner against the larger development of
the play as a whole.

There are many other cases in Elizabethan drama where it is
impossible to be certain whether the actor is speaking monologue or dialogue, and what kind of behaviour is represented by
the speech. Failure to realize this has led some critics to wonder
unnecessarily as to the meaning of Cleopatra's 'apostrophe' (I. v):

> Thinke on me
> That am with Phoebus amorous pinches blacke,
> And wrinkled deepe in time.

Capell punctuated this passage as a question, making Antony
the subject of 'think'. In the Arden edition R. H. Case suggests
that, as an alternative, one might suppose the Queen to be addressing Charmian. In this case, 'Think on me' is to be taken as
meaning 'Just imagine! it is me he loves!'[1] But there is no need
to look for an interlocutor; this apostrophizing of an absent lover
is merely the expression of Cleopatra's exultation in his love. It is
only when we assume that the words must always represent what
can be said or thought in real life that we can even begin to make
the mistake of interpreting these lines as dialogue, or be disturbed
at finding that they might be monologue. Another example of
apostrophe in the same play is equally hard to identify as either

---

[1] R. H. Case, *Antony and Cleopatra* (1938), p. 35 and note. H. H. Furness,
The Tragedy of Antony and Cleopatra (1907), p. 72 and note.

dialogue or monologue: any attempt to do so at once raises irrelevant issues. Caesar, in Rome, invokes the memory of Antony in an earlier, more Spartan-like role than that in which we have seen him in this play (I. iv).

> *Anthony*,
>
> .   .   .   .
>
> .   .   .   at thy heele
> Did Famine follow, whom thou fought'st against,
> (Though daintily brought vp) with patience more
> Then Sauages could suffer.

As the speech ends Lepidus, who is standing by throughout, observes in agreement, ''Tis pitty of him'. As Caesar has been overheard, his speech cannot represent silent soliloquy. Nevertheless, he is not speaking dialogue to Lepidus. The apostrophe is a passionate figure, which creates for us an understanding of that earlier, hardier Antony, now apparently no more. A heroic presence is evoked, to be contrasted sadly with the unheroic person whom we have seen in Egypt: we, too, feel ''Tis pitty of him'.

We must be prepared to respond to Elizabethan drama in the same attitude of mind as we respond to opera or ballet before we can hope to criticize the dramatists' techniques justly. In opera the singer must give all his care to communicating what has been expressed by the composer in music: and we ought not to demand from a performer a larger element of impersonation, a more realistic imitation of actual behaviour, than is needed to achieve the artist's purpose. If, for instance, Mozart's purpose had included a realistic imitation of a duel in *Don Giovanni*, he need not have used music and song to create the scene as it stands; he could have dispensed with singing and with the orchestra. The fact that he has used voices and instruments to express what he is imagining about the situation, makes it necessary for us to respond to them if we are to imagine the story in his terms. Thus, careful attention to the business of realistic duelling can only be at the expense of correct performance; and only correct performance can communicate to us in the theatre what was in Mozart's mind. We are not asked to suspend our disbelief in a race of men and women who communicate by song to the everlasting accompaniment of an orchestra. It would be a mistake to consider that whenever a performer sings we are to interpret what we hear as representing what could be spoken audibly or thought silently in real life. We have merely to allow ourselves, by means of a complex response to singing and orchestral music, to create in our minds an intellectual and emotional understanding of what has been imagined by the artist. And part of our complex response is to an element in the work of art which cannot be interpreted as anything but a communication of what is in the artist's mind. More often than not the performers need to give all their attention to their singing; they have to face the audience and make certain that the exact quality of the composer's music is appreciated. There is no possibility of a successful compromise between the measures necessary to represent the audible and visible surfaces of life, on the one hand, and the correct way of performing a scene in opera, on the other, where song is designed to affect us in virtue of the fact that it is song.

The Elizabethan dramatist used language to affect his audience without attempting to disguise the fact that the language was his. In the theatre it was the performer's business to communicate by means of *actio* all the literary quality of the lines, whether these were verse or prose. The actor then, like the opera-singer to-day, had to preserve a balance between performance and impersonation. In his *Über die Bestimmung der Oper* Richard Wagner refers to the difficulty experienced by singers when they imagine a situation too realistically. He quotes the case of Schröder-Devrient who, in *Fidelio*, did not sing but 'positively *spoke*—and with a terrible accent of despair—the last word of the phrase—"another step—and thou art—DEAD" '.[1] It is even more difficult, to-day, for an actor to speak Elizabethan dramatic verse and prose without making the same kind of mistake. As in

[1] Tr. B. H. Clark, *European Theories of Drama* (1929), p. 351.

opera the claims of singing come first, so in Elizabethan drama those of language must first be satisfied. In each case correct performance includes an element of impersonation; but this should not be allowed to obscure a just appreciation of the artist's use of his medium; for it is by his use of that medium that he can make us imagine with his mind. In the case of the first meeting of Romeo and Juliet it is essential for the theatre audience to respond to the literary quality of the lines. If these are imagined primarily as representing dialogue which could be interchanged between a pair of romantic lovers, each inspired to heights of poetry, the scene cannot achieve its fullest effect. For these lines are written in the form of a sonnet, and no attempt at representing dialogue must be allowed to prevent this particular arrangement of sounds and rhythms reacting upon the audience. The combination of figures of word and thought within the pattern of the sonnet-form records complexities of meaning and emotion which were involved for Shakespeare in this scene as he imagined it in relation to the whole of the story.

What the Prologue has to tell about the enmity between two noble families is confirmed by the opening of the play. Strict decorum in the portrayal of rank and vocation would make the participants in the brawl appear almost as representatives of the different estates in the structure of society in Verona. First come the coarse swaggering retainers, dressed in the livery of their respective houses. The nature of their puns, the very method of provoking conflict, proclaim their ignobility. According to Bulwer, 'if we see one bite his Thumbe at us we soon infer he meanes us no good'.[1] This sign of anger goes well with the generally unpolished behaviour of the serving-men, which is so much in contrast with the dash and verve of Benvolio and Tybalt. The brawl which started among the commoners swiftly absorbs the noblemen; and the extent to which this canker of dissension is eating into Verona is measured by the appearance of the heads of the families themselves, with their ladies, to add threatening

[1] *Chirol.*, p. 160.

cries to the clamour on the stage. Set against this picture of dis-
cord, we see the sound element, the citizens determined to preserve order, setting upon both sides with their clubs, the citizen
weapon. Then silence—before the majesty of the state, represented by the massive dignity of the Prince who so obviously
commands instant respect. As the stage is emptying we hear
Romeo named for the first time. Old Montague is perturbed at
the 'black and portentous' humour which has taken possession
of his son.

I do not think there is any justification for the modern attitude
of playful mirth towards the agony of Romeo's unrequited love.
There is nothing of merriment in Benvolio's description of the
early-morning scene; and Montague expresses an anxiety which
is to be taken seriously, with his reference to the

> bud bit with an enuious worme
> Ere he can spread his sweete leaues to the ayre,
> Or dedicate his beauty to the same.

This in truth is Romeo, when we see him for the first time. Far
gone in the melancholy of love, his posture is dejected, with
wreathed arms, and lowered gaze, and accompanied with sighs,
all betokening a disintegration of spirit as the result of a fruitless
love for the vain chastity of Rosaline. We, like Benvolio, should
feel no incentive to laughter; Romeo's frantic attempts to describe the emptiness of the love within him, its uselessness and
futility, are deadly earnest. His verses here are not to be con-
fused with the bubbling-over of a mind rich in conceits, such as
we encounter later from Mercutio. 'Mis-shapen chaos of well-
seeming forms' is an accurate expression of what existence itself
must seem to a man in Romeo's state of soul: here, in fact, is the
sickness of the spirit which Polonius diagnoses in Hamlet. But
this is Romeo before his meeting with Juliet; and to appreciate
the essence of their relationship when it develops it is necessary
to understand that his early and unheroic dejection, like that of
Samson in Milton's poem, is painted with such emphasis, only
that we shall be able to mark the difference when it gives way to
the normal behaviour expected of a heroic personage.

Thus, with apprehension of ill to come, Romeo goes reluc-
tantly to the festivities at the enemy's house. And here, for the
first time, Shakespeare reassures us that somewhere beneath
the seeming irregularity there is an ordered pattern. Here,
with the head of the House of Capulet hospitably welcoming his
guests, there is recreation for our eyes and ears, in harmony and
concord of the dance. This is performed with an air of dignified
gaiety; it is an expression of that solemn *allegria* celebrated later
by Milton when he banished hence a loathed Melancholy in
order to bid welcome to a 'Goddess fair and free'. It is possible,
though we cannot be certain, that the Elizabethan audience
would be reminded at this moment that the dance could be
interpreted as a symbol of the fundamental harmony of the
universe: some of the spectators may even have read into the
individual movements the allegorical meanings mentioned by
Elyot in *The Governor*, when he speaks of dancing as a coming
together of male and female virtues. Even without these deeper
implications, however, the dance in the house of the Capulets
must impress us with a sense of orderliness such as we have not
experienced at any earlier moment in the play. It seems therefore
fitting that Romeo's first glimpse of Juliet brings from him the
decision:

> The measure done, Ile watch her place of stand,
> And touching hers, make blessed my rude hand.

There is a sudden surging up of violence: disorder flares in
Tybalt's passion. But the head of the family asserts himself, and
order is maintained: not, however, without our having been
reminded of the hatred and malevolence which stand between
Romeo and the attainment of his bliss. When the measure is
ended all depart, except Romeo and Juliet, who draw nearer to
one another for their first exchange of love.

The full purpose of the lines given to the actors can only be
appreciated when the sonnet is subjected to a literary analysis.
In its rhyming it follows the 'English' model, a form firmly
associated with the treatment of love. Normally a sonnet treats
one idea through three successive stages. First the idea is put

forward from one point of view, taking up the first eight lines, the octave. Then, at the pause, or *volta*, it is possible to introduce another aspect, which is treated briefly before the declaration of what is sometimes called 'an intellectual conclusion' in the last line or last two lines of the poem. Thus we might say that a theme is given out and treated in the octave; and a new development takes place, to be succeeded by a resolution, in the sestet.

Here the octave consists of two quatrains. Romeo speaks the first with the rhyme-scheme 'hand—this—stand—kiss'. Juliet replies in the next: and now the rhymes are 'much—this—touch —kiss'. At the *volta* there is a change of rhyme. The sestet consists of a quatrain and a couplet. Romeo speaks the first line, only one being spoken by Juliet in the quatrain, whilst they each have one in the couplet. He is allotted eight, and she six, of the fourteen lines that go to make the sonnet. In the first quatrain he asks to kiss her hand, receiving the reply in the next four lines that he must rest content with the 'palmer's kiss'. Thus checked he tries again, and the new rhyme-scheme allows of a little more plaintive urgency on his part. But despite the fact that Romeo speaks most of the lines in the sestet, it is Juliet who prevails: he is granted a kiss only when he has in effect accepted her terms by falling to his knees and admitting that holiness, not profanity, shall rule in their relationship. We must remember that Romeo is dressed as a palmer, and that his name itself means pilgrim— 'one who goes to Rome'. She looks like a saint at whose shrine he comes to worship, and the imagery of these fourteen lines emphasizes this aspect of their love.

Gently and reverently he touches her hand, attempting to raise it to his lips as he comes to the last line of the first quatrain:

> To smooth that rough touch, with a tender kisse.

But she restrains him gently and graciously, pointing out that her hand needs no such compensation for his touch, stressing the mannerliness of his devotion, so long as it is confined to touching her hand, not kissing it: and, disengaging her fingers from his grip, to lay her hand lightly on his, she adds:

> For Saints haue hands, that Pilgrims hands do tuch,
> And palme to palme is holy Palmers kisse.

With the change of rhyme Romeo asks again, sounding out the open vowels of 'too' and 'do' with that sweet tuning of the voice which renaissance writers allot to the pronouncing of figures of words. Again he is diverted as she tells him he must use his lips in prayer. Still touching her hand he begs, 'let lips do what hands do', and putting both his hands together in an attitude of prayer,

> They pray (grant thou) least faith turne to dispaire.

We have now reached the couplet: at first, in a posture of denial, Juliet insists, 'Saints do not move'. But, as he goes on his knees in full humility, she adds, 'But grant for prayer's sake'. The resolution has come, to be confirmed in the last line of the sonnet, as Romeo, rising from his knees, states rather than begs:

> Then moue not while my prayers effect I take.

Then, and not until this moment, does he kiss her.

Shakespeare's purpose can only be achieved if his audience is allowed to respond to the figures, the images, and the metrical pattern of these fourteen lines. There is no need to imitate dialogue realistically: but there is every necessity for speaking the lines so that the rhymes are heard, and the poet's experience shared. He has refined the essential meaning which the lovers' relationship expressed for him, infusing this essence into fourteen lines, which are of overwhelming intensity, and yet gracious and restrained.

Although the lovers are star-crossed, once brought together their own characters take a hand in determining the details of their fate. As the fourteen lines of their first meeting are pronounced it is apparent that Juliet stands as a saint towards her lover. As the voices declaim alternately, the sweet repetitions of the rhyme, the benign grace of the 'action', mingle in a harmony of sound and gesture. The apt conceits, the playing upon the terms 'pilgrim', 'saint', 'life', 'hands', 'prayer', work upon us like a ritual of love and adoration, in which gallantry is purged of all arrogance, and humility is fired with passion. Rhetorical acting allows the words alone to guide the actors, so that from their sounds and movements the scene takes shape before us, and its meaning is impressed upon the mind. Juliet regenerates her lover: the dejected green-sick youth has gone.

To enable the sonnet to achieve its full effect in the theatre there is no need for the actors to speak to one another as in the dialogue of real life. If they speak their lines to the auditorium we, as is the case in opera, can imagine dialogue in Shakespeare's terms. Indeed, it is by no means certain that the modern method of speaking dialogue was even known to Shakespeare's stage. When the naturalist movement reached its climax in the last quarter of the nineteenth century, reformers of the drama all over Europe found that it was necessary to train actors not to speak dialogue 'out front', but to turn and stand with the back to the audience in order to fulfil the requirements of consistent realism.

Our modern actors simulate conversation as realistically as possible, even in verse-plays. As a result we find it hard to imagine a performance as satisfactory when the dialogue is spoken towards the audience. Yet in the music-hall we are accustomed to-day to the spectacle of two performers engaged in 'cross-talk', which is superficially dialogue, but which does not require the performers to face and speak to one another as in naturalistic conversation. The Elizabethan dramatist did not rely for his effects upon the ability of his audience to recognize, nor upon that of his performers to simulate, dialogue or 'mental' or 'verbal' soliloquy. As Sir Richard Baker insists, it is irrelevant to charge dramatists with lying or deceit: 'For, seeing that, which they do, is not done to *Circumvent*, but to *Represent*; not to *Deceive* others, but to make others *Conceive*.'[1] And Sidney's *Apologie* makes the same point: 'The Poet neuer maketh any

---

[1] Baker, op. cit., pp. 21–2.

circles about your imagination, to coniure you to beleeue for true what he writes.' If children are not deceived at the sight of 'Thebes written in great Letters vpon an olde doore', there is obviously no sense in attacking poets as deceivers of grown men.[1] The popular dramatists and the neo-classicists alike believed that the audience was affected by the power of language.

This attitude to dramatic poetry produces lines which are robbed of their effect if spoken as dialogue between the actors on the stage. When Cleomenes and Dion return from Delphos, for instance, in The Winter's Tale, if we insist on regarding their speeches primarily as dialogue, we are left with a dull scene of éclaircissement; to let us know where they have been, and what they saw and did there, Shakespeare has contrived somewhat inartistically, it seems, that each shall tell the other what both already know. It is possible to forget the flaws when reading and enjoying the verse. But in the modern theatre, where the actors try to appear in realistic conversation, the scene sags. Nevertheless, there is no reason to believe that Shakespeare faltered here. Once again we have not to do with true dialogue, but with a sequence of alternate declamation. Instead of being bored by a pair of tedious travellers, we should be inspired by what is almost antiphonal chanting to imagine the wonder and the majesty of their experience on the island. We, too, are amazed by the thunder, the pomp of the ceremony awes us, and we feel as if we had been there with them, instead of sharing in the agony at Leontes' court. By the time that this scene is over we are prepared emotionally to react as the dramatist had reacted towards Hermione's trial and the punishment inflicted by the angry god.

Whilst it has not yet been possible to state the grounds of criticism valid in Elizabethan drama, nevertheless an understanding of the acting and of the traditional attitude to dramatic poetry with which actio was associated enables us to avoid some of the mistakes which must inevitably follow the application of standards which are not relevant. A speech is not necessarily to

[1] An Apology for Poetry (1595), ed. Gregory Smith, i. 185.

be judged as a representation of something which might happen in actual life. And in estimating the skill with which a dramatist has constructed his play we should rather examine each speech or scene as a contribution towards the expressing of all that he has imagined about his story and about the people who take part in it. It does not matter whether he has used speeches that can be interpreted as dialogue, 'mental' or 'verbal' soliloquy, or the kind of monologue known as 'direct address' which cannot be interpreted as representing anything that occurs outside a play or poem. What matters is the additional insight into the meaning of the story, the additional piece of information which makes us react as it develops: if these are given at the right moment, then it is irrelevant to deplore the fact that monologue may have been used: and this irrelevancy becomes more obvious when we reflect that Elizabethan acting did not make our modern distinction between monologue and dialogue. We have seen this in the examples which have already been treated. But as these have been cases in which modern critics and commentators usually find something amiss with the dramatist's technique, it may be thought that I propose to invoke the aid of renaissance acting and dramatic theory only as a crutch to the Elizabethans' halting muse. We should, however, recognize that even where we normally believe the dramatist to have succeeded, it is possible to transform our vision of a play, and thus our criticism, by ignoring the modern standards usually taken for granted, and by imagining instead with the eyes of an Elizabethan audience. And no better example can be found than Shakespeare's *Hamlet*.

The structure of *Hamlet* is normally considered to be the play's weakest point: but in the light of Elizabethan acting we discover a fast-moving plot of action and mystery, which is saved from becoming melodramatic by the author's ability to draw character, and his poetic apprehension of the implications underlying a story in some respects almost as barbarous as that of *Titus Andronicus*. A survey of the first three scenes is enough to substantiate this statement, to show how Shakespeare has shaped his play, launching it with as superb a piece of exposition as is to be found in the whole of drama. But we cannot possibly appreciate his technique if we persist in maintaining the modern distinctions between speech to oneself and speech to another, and in thinking of the play as performed in a modern theatre. We must also forget to think of 'direct address' as breaking the bounds between the play-world and the real world. In Elizabethan drama, as in the epic, no such conception is possible; the players do not create a play-world, any more than the words of epic create an epic world, distinct from that inhabited by reader and audience. In one case the printed words, and in the other the 'animated' words, induce us to imagine the story for ourselves. The player does not break into the world of actuality when he speaks 'direct address': he cannot emerge from the play-world to address us, as that world only exists in the imagination. Whatever is done by the actor, whether he speaks what we call monologue or what we call dialogue, is done solely for our benefit, so that we shall be enabled to imagine. Finally, in order to appreciate what Shakespeare has done in this first act, it is also necessary for us to empty our minds of all that we know about the play, and to imagine ourselves utterly ignorant of the characters and story.

The first scene sets us asking questions: the possibility of one explanation is suggested in the next, to be contradicted in the third. Why, as the play opens, is the atmosphere so tense that a soldier, coming on to mount guard, raps out a challenge to the sentry about to go off duty? What is the reason for the appearance of this Ghost? Our first sight of it is of a majestic, noble figure, clad cap-à-pie in a slightly antiquated fashion of armour. With the stride of a hero and the superb bearing of a renaissance monarch at the head of his army, it passes silently before the men on the platform. As the Ghost goes 'slow and stately' by, its royalty dwarfs them: we perceive in their behaviour a respect for the nobility of both spirit and bearing with which we too are impressed as we watch the proceedings on the stage. In its short respite from purgatory the Ghost resents the importunities of its former subjects, and stalks off proudly when charged to answer. Horatio, Marcellus, and Bernardo, in their conversation, now inform us of warlike preparations to meet the threat from Fortinbras. And when the Ghost comes on again, as the result of Horatio's questioning, we are able to wonder whether it walks until some 'good thing be done' to do it ease; or whether it has been disturbed by some foreknowledge of its country's fate. Each of these reasons could supply a perfectly valid explanation for the spirit's presence; and we know that Denmark seems on the verge of war. There is, however, yet another possibility; perhaps the Ghost has been attracted from its grave by hoarded treasure 'in the womb of earth'. But we are left to puzzle; for as the last question is put to it—in Horatio's later words—

> It lifted vp it head and did addresse
> It selfe to motion, like as it would speake.

There the Ghost stands, arm upraised for attention, its proud and haughty gaze turned upwards. There is a pause, as it prepares to speak, to put an end to uncertainty and let us know the reason for its coming. The right hand comes down, to go out from the trunk in an action accompanying the opening words; and as all its regal woe comes into its eyes—more 'in sorrow than in anger', yet there is some anger—we sense the muscles moving, the lips about to open; then in the place of an eerie silence we are aware suddenly of the singing of a cock, crowing from afar through the clear morning air. This call is often counted as ridiculous to-day: this is perhaps because its use in *Peter Pan* has made us incapable of imagining the full beauty of a cock-crow. Perhaps, too, we have forgotten that when a cock is heard in the silence of the country-side, and from a distance, it sings in a clear, pure, celestial voice that truly deserves the name of *chaunteclair*. That is how I imagine the cock crowing in *Hamlet*; and as it crows the spirit is transformed. Gone is the proud and martial arrogance; gone the king who overawes his subjects: in his place a hunted wretch cowers abjectly, crouching as the sound hits him: he quivers, writhing and imploring as if the furies themselves stood over him with whips. As Horatio says:

> it started, like a guilty thing
> Vpon a fearfull Summons.

As the Ghost becomes a hunted thing its former subjects turn to hunters. But in the scuffle, as they close on it, the Ghost is gone. For one appalling moment, as the bird sang the night's passing, we witnessed a spirit in torment. Was it a soul that needed easing, or was it a devil, a guilty thing, come in search of treasure in the caves of the earth, or to revel in the prospect of Danish misery? Much is done at this moment to make us understand the reality of Hamlet's doubts whether he should take the Ghost's word alone as proof of his uncle's guilt. And when we know later that the elder Hamlet had been murdered, the memory of this agony on the platform leads us to sympathize with the raging pity which the crime has inspired within his son. But now, as the first scene closes, with Horatio and the soldiers resolved to seek out the Prince, we are left with the knowledge that 'It was about to speak, when the cock crew', and that it seemed disposed to answer only when asked if it had come back for hidden gold.

The next scene suggests to us very skilfully that the Ghost has not returned to cry for vengeance against the king now on the throne. Claudius is made to seem wholly admirable: he seems to have that quality of heroic amiableness which wins all hearts. He even has time to interest himself in the family affairs of a trusted adviser; and our first impression is of a Denmark in good hands, which can be trusted to preserve it in any future trials. There is, however, one discordant note in this harmony of mutual congratulation—the proud, black-clad figure of the Prince. Now it is important to forget the Hamlet of the modern theatre. We have to imagine a man of superb bearing, who contrives to suggest a contempt and scorn for the 'uses' of a world not worthy of his interest. He is wholly concerned with his grief; his mind is turned in on itself; but his brooding is obviously dangerous. His arrogance expresses itself silently, but none the less insultingly. Two facts are clear: first, that the Danes could hardly rely on him to govern them in this humour in the face of threats from Norway: and second, he radiates contempt for all who take part in the colourful ceremony of Claudius's court.

When all other business is finished Claudius turns to win his nephew over. And, as he tries to persuade Hamlet, the King really states his case to us. In the common-sense of daylight, in the face of the court's adulation, of the Queen's radiant happiness in her new husband's love, recognizing the truth of the reproach to Hamlet, who hardly appears to advantage, we wonder whether there is anything seriously wrong with Denmark to justify the Ghost's appearance. And now Gertrude adds her voice to her husband's appeals to the Prince: and this, I believe, is a turning-point in the scene. Hamlet has been out-manœuvred to a position in which he must either give way or discredit himself in the eyes of the Danes. Although modern opinion is against me, I believe that at this moment he finds a way out in recognizing the fact that Gertrude is his mother, and conceding gracefully to her what pride and honour withhold when the supplicant is Claudius. I believe that Hamlet's behaviour changes now: that he treats nis mother to what Claudius rightly describes as 'a loving and a fair reply', accompanied by the grace and courtesy of one who is described as having been 'the mould of form'. The tension is broken: the courtiers who have stood by, fearful of a violent family quarrel—which rank could make a public disaster—now relax and breathe more freely. Claudius seems to have reason for his gaiety. The last vestige of gloom is conquered: a great feast is planned by a monarch who seems the personification of the magnificence of spirit valued by the renaissance in its monarchs. Here again, let us pause to remember that we still do not know that he is a plausible villain. We do not yet know him as the perfect hypocrite: we know him only as he seems, as one who can give telling reasons to justify himself, reasons which weigh with us and can convince us, so long as we do not know that they hide rather than reveal his actual motives.

And now, whilst we hover between decisions, still puzzled as to the moral issues, and not quite certain, such is Shakespeare's skill, whether Hamlet is going to be shown as the enemy of his uncle, the Prince, in monologue, brings the play's exposition almost to its end.

I believe that we ought not to look upon Hamlet's first monologue as 'mental soliloquy' and no more. It is true that the speech may represent a silent soliloquy; but when the lines were declaimed in the rhetorical manner, I do not think that the spectators were conscious so much of what kind of actual behaviour was represented as of the emotion which was being expressed, and of the light thrown on the situation in the play by the reasons which Hamlet gives for his emotion. In other words, we are made to understand Hamlet's position and emotions at this stage of the story by an author who can imagine this particular situation as involving doubts and uncertainties for all who lack his own omniscience. The monologue falls into two sections. In the first our actor makes us conceive of the intense grief and despair of humanity which Shakespeare imagined in the Prince's mind. But the opening *invocatio* must not be interpreted as a longing for suicide. On the contrary, as the first four lines are pronounced, we realize that there is no possibility of self-murder: in that certainty lies the fullness of the anguish. No way out of the situation can be seen at this point. By means of what has been called 'the rhetoric of impossibles' one impossibility, that the 'too too solid Flesh' could melt, is balanced against a known certainty, that self-slaughter is forbidden. We may not yet agree with Hamlet's opinion of the world, but, despite his answer to his mother, we know that for him the world is still 'an unweeded Garden'.

In the second part of this speech the actor has not merely to act Hamlet's 'passion', he has also to expound Hamlet's view of affairs in Denmark; and in such a way that we start to reverse our opinion of Claudius. When we have heard why Hamlet is disgusted with the world, we, too, feel that his mood is justified, that an evil influence seems to be blinding a whole nation to facts that really stand out plain. Here, we are told, is a king, dead but two months, and the whole court has forgotten him, giving itself up happily to the thought of a great feast this very night: and, as if that were not enough, the dead king's son has just been reprimanded in public for mourning his father, so recently lost. Moreover, that father was 'so excellent a King', a man in every way superior to his successor, who has himself impressed us with his greatness of spirit. But the court could not wait two months before it turned again to feasting, and the widow could not even wait one month before remarrying. Perhaps, we might say to ourselves, she did not love her first husband; but Hamlet sweeps away this facile explanation. For Gertrude

> would hang on him,
> As if encrease of Appetite had growne
> By what it fed on.

The facts do not make sense; or if they do, it is only in a world which is, indeed, possessed by 'things rank and gross in Nature'. For the indecorum of Gertrude's behaviour has deepened into unnatural sin. If we analyse the structure of the speech we cannot fail to perceive how Hamlet repeats his points, comes back to them like counsel for the prosecution who will not let us overlook a disconcerting piece of evidence: and, for fear we may be inclined to explain away what he says as too subjective a view of events, he brings us up sharply with a reminder which must make us pause: after all, the second marriage was 'within a month', and Claudius himself spoke of 'one Auspicious, and Dropping eye'.

Hamlet has only to remind us of facts which nobody has attempted to hide: but when a skilled actor has pronounced his words with horror and disgust we, with him, must confess our failure to comprehend how no one else in Denmark can be aware of the real significance of those facts. We share Hamlet's loathing and bewilderment. We feel that a world which accepts the situation with more than acquiescence, with exultation, must be rotten at the core. We do not pity Hamlet from without; our reason, our logic, our sense of right and wrong, our loathing and hatred of tyranny and evil, all cry out for justice: 'It is not, nor it cannot come to good.'

But here the speaker stops and considers things as they are, recognizing that as yet there is nothing he can do; his country-men are so possessed of evil.

> But breake my heart, for I must hold my tongue.

It seems at this moment that Claudius has won. Hamlet can do nothing: he must play the loving son, willy nilly: there is nothing else left that he can do. And at this point the last stage of the exposition of the main plot begins to develop. Horatio arrives with his fellow watchers to tell the Prince what they have seen. He resolves to wait upon the battlements with them to see the Ghost if it appears. And in case we have not understood the moral issues which underlie a conflict between Claudius and Hamlet, Shakespeare has summed up for us the theme of his play in the *sententia* whose couplet brings the scene to a close:

> foule deeds will rise,
> Though all the earth orewhelm them to mens eies.

With these rhymes ringing in our ears, we realize what is in-volved. The forces of darkness, using Claudius and a blind, un-imaginative world, are trying to obstruct divine justice. A wrong has been done, but the wrongdoer is unpunished. When the Ghost came, it could not speak. To the world there is nothing amiss: apparently Claudius has succeeded his brother in every detail. Queen, court, Hamlet—all have accepted him. And then the pull comes from the other side. Hamlet proves to us that his uncle only seems to have inherited all the dead king's temporal and spiritual possessions. The acclamation of this court is poisoned; the splendour of her first husband's relationship with Gertrude has been replaced by the degradation of an incestuous lust. And, for a son's genuine love, the new king has a nephew's hate disguised.

The skill which Shakespeare has exercised in the structure of this play becomes apparent to the reader who asks what each scene or passage—whether monologue or dialogue—does, rather than what kind of behaviour it represents. And what is possible for the reader attentive to the disposition and elocution of the literary text, was equally possible for the spectator, when the play was performed in the Elizabethan manner.

I am conscious of the fact that I have not answered any questions here, though perhaps I have demonstrated that some are irrelevant: nor have I set up new standards. It has rather been my purpose in this chapter to suggest new methods of approach which may reveal the answer and determine the standards. It is clear that we must try to expel prejudices of which we are often unconscious, in order to imagine a scene as is necessary to ensure an understanding of Elizabethan technique. And no criticism, however subtly academic or brutally practical, can be entirely valid if it ignores the original effect in the theatre of lines 'animated with action' by the Elizabethan players.

VII

THE POEM AND THE THEATRE

SAMUEL JOHNSON has often been criticized for the inadequacy of his assertion that in his day people went to the theatre 'to hear a certain number of lines recited with just gesture and elegant modulation'.[1] It is very true that modern audiences require more than this when they go to see a play: nevertheless, in Johnson's time there would be little disagreement with his statement from those who understood the fundamentals of dramatic art. And I have no doubt that he would have secured the hearty concurrence of those Elizabethans who flocked to the play-house. We have the assurance of Sir Richard Baker that the most enjoyable performances which he could remember were those in which Burbage or Alleyn took part. The Elizabethan playgoer was drawn to the theatre to enjoy their grace of voice and action.

For, it is not the scurrility, and ribaldry, that gives the contentment, ... but it is the *Ingeniousness* of the Speech, when it is fitted to the Person; and the *Gracefulness* of the *Action*, when it is fitted to the Speech; and therefore a Play *read*, hath not half the pleasure of a Play *Acted*: for though it have the pleasure of *ingenious Speeches*; yet it wants the pleasure of *Gracefull action*: and we may well acknowledg, that *Gracefulness* of *action*, is the greatest pleasure of a *Play*; seeing it is the greatest pleasure of (the Art of pleasure) *Rhetorick*: in which we may be bold to say; there never had been so good Oratours, if there had not first been Players: seeing the best Oratours that ever were, account it no shame, to have learned the gracefulness of their Action, even from Players: *Demosthenes* from *Satyrus*; and *Cicero* from *Roscius*.[2]

Whilst Baker gives enjoyment of 'pronunciation' as the great attraction of the theatre, he is still careful to insist that there is no essential difference between a play read and the same play performed in the theatre. 'And what doth a Player else, but

---

[1] Preface to *Shakespeare* (1765), I. xxvii.
[2] Baker, op. cit., pp. 34–5.

onely say that without book, which we may read within Book ?'[1]
This is very near Johnson's 'a dramatick exhibition is a book
recited with concomitants that encrease or diminish its effect'.[2]

For Baker and his age, acting was such that the effect of the
book was increased; the extra pleasure of performance resulted
from the animation of words by voice and gesture which communicated the full quality of the writer's use of language. But
by Johnson's time actors were no longer capable of impersonat-
ing character and still doing justice to the *elocutio* of their lines.
And so he laments that 'imperial tragedy' was weaker in the
eighteenth-century theatre than on the printed page. When
reading a play it was possible to perceive and appreciate the
beauties and sublimities which were inevitably lost in performance. 'The humour of *Petruchio* may be heightened by grimace;
but what voice or what gesture can hope to add dignity or force
to the soliloquy of *Cato*.' In Shakespeare's day each of these
feats could have been accomplished by an actor trained in
rhetorical delivery. But Johnson, like Lamb, could create for
himself when reading a poetic intensity which was absent from
the recitation of an actor in the theatre. Each of these critics felt
that a play should provide them with a literary experience in the
theatre no less than in the study. In this desire they were at one
with Baker and the Elizabethans for whom a play performed was
a literary experience, just as for us an opera—however full of
incident its plot—is still, when performed, a musical experience.
It is true that *Hamlet* is a different kind of experience from
Paradise Lost, but so is *The Magic Flute* from the Kreuzer
Sonata. The difference between the play and the epic is a difference between two kinds of literature, not one between two
different arts.

To-day we feel that a printed play is a poor substitute for one
performed in the theatre. Provided his work succeeds there, we
credit the playwright with success, however poor the literary
quality of his lines judged by literary standards. But the Elizabethans did not distinguish as we do between acted drama, and

---

[1] Baker, op. cit., p. 43.   [2] Op. cit., I. xxix.

drama read in the study: and for many, success in the theatre did not compensate for failure in the study. However successful a play might have been in performance, they judged its value by literary standards none the less. If found deficient by these standards, then its author merited censure. The popular playwrights themselves seem to have agreed as to the validity of such judgement. For in Prefaces and Letters Dedicatory they are at pains to assert their own awareness of the faults of their work. Webster makes the following apology for his *The Devil's Lawcase*, addressed to 'The Juditious Reader': 'I am so farre from praising my selfe, that I have not giuen way to divers of my Friends, whose unbeg'd Commendatory Verses offered themselves to doe me service in the Front of this Poeme. A great part of the grace of this (I confesse) lay in Action: yet can no Action ever be gracious, where the decency of the Language, and Ingenious structure of the Scæne, arrive not to make up a perfect Harmony.'[1]

He knew that when his play went into print it would be judged according to its language, and to the skill or clumsiness shown in structure. *Actio* could hide the flaws in a play, just as it could distract attention from those of an oration. In *The Alphabet of Tales* we may read: 'a grete parte of Demostenes wantys whan it is red, more than when it is hard.' This is included in a section headed: 'Predicacio cum bono modo et gestu multum valet.'[2] Thomas Wright assures us: 'I haue seene some preachers very meane schollers, . . . yet for that they excelled in action all the world followed them.'[3] And the same point, naturally, is stressed by Bulwer, who relates that on one occasion Queen Elizabeth had been so impressed by a sermon preached in her presence that she asked for the text, in order to read it at her leisure. But, on reading it herself, she found that without the aid of the preacher's delivery it was 'one of the best Sermons She ever heard, and the worst she ever read'.[4]

---

[1] *Works*, ed. Lucas (1927), ii. 236.
[2] *The Alphabet of Tales*, ed. Macleod Banks (1905), ii. 426.
[3] *The Passions of the Mind*, p. 176.   [4] *Chiron.*, pp. 6–7.

Aware that his play could excite a similar comment from a reader, although *actio* would hide its worst faults from a spectator, Webster is anxious to make quite clear that his mistakes have not been the result of ignorance but of expediency. 'If it be objected this is no true Drammaticke Poem, I shall easily confesse it,' he observes in a statement 'To the Reader' prefixed to *The White Devil*; and adds '*non potes in nugas dicere plura meas: Ipse ego quam dixi*, willingly and not ignorantly, in this kind have I faulted'. And in thus taking 'that liberty, which other men have taken before me', Webster admitted that he did not observe 'all the criticall laws', there being no necessity to do so when entertaining the incapable multitude.[1]

Another popular dramatist, Marston, admits his failure by serious critical standards in an address 'To the Reader' to be found before his *Parasitaster, Or the Fawne* (1606). 'If any shall wonder why I print a Comedie, whose life rests much in the Actors voice: Let such know, that it cannot auoide publishing: let it therefore stand with good excuse, that I haue been my owne setter out.' He adds in a note on the next page: '*Comedies*, are writ to be spoken, not read: Remember the life of these things consists in action.' This can be misread as a determined insistence that plays ought to be written solely with a view to success in the theatre, irrespective of their quality as literature. But really, all Marston is making is the simple statement that the popular play is faulty because its author relies too much on *actio* to 'animate' his text in the theatre. This is a plea for compassion rather than a defence. And Marston promises 'for your courteous suruay of my pen, I will present a Tragedy to you which shall abide the most curious perusall'.[2] Again, he begs for tolerance from the reader of *The Malcontent* (1604):

I would faine leave the paper; onely one thing afflicts mee, to thinke that scenes inuented, meerely to be spoken, should be inforcively published to be read . . . but I shal intreat . . . that the vnhandsome shape which this trifle in reading presents, may bee pardoned, for the

---

[1] *Works*, ed. Lucas, i. 107, 108.
[2] Sigs. A2^r, A2^v.

pleasure it once afforded you, when it was presented with the soule of lively action.[1]

John Ford's 'To the deserving Memory of this Worthy Worke, and the Author, Mr. PHILIP MASSINGER' was inspired by the latter's *The Great Duke of Florence* (1636); this play, Ford insists, succeeded on its merits as dramatic poetry and not as the result of the gloss given by acting.

> Action gives many Poems right to live,
> This Piece gave life to Action; and will give
> For state, and language, in each change of Age,
> To Time, delight; and honour to the stage.[2]

Massinger's *A New Way to Pay Old Debts* (1633) is celebrated in a dedicatory poem which compares him to Beaumont and Fletcher, continuing

> if you loue not praise
> You must forbeare the publishing of playes.
> The craftie Mazes of the cunning plot;
> The polish'd phrase; the sweet expressions; got
> Neither by theft, nor violence; the conceipt
> Fresh, and vnsullied; All is of weight,
> Able to make the captiue Reader know
> I did but iustice when I plac't you so.

And the writer of a poem 'on his *Emperor of the East*' (1632),[3] bids him

> still write
> Poems like this, that can indure the light,
> And search of abler iudgements. This will raise
> Thy Name, the others Scandall is thy praise.
> This oft perus'd by graue witts, shall liue long,
> Not dye as soone, as pass'd the Actors tongue,
> (The fate of slighter toyes) And I must say
> 'Tis not enough to make a passing play,
> In a true Poet. [4]

The attitude of the pre-Restoration writers and public towards a play as a dramatic poem is summed up in the Address

---

[1] Sig. A4^r.   [2] Sig. A4^v.   [3] Sig. A3^v.   [4] Sig. A4^r.

to the Reader of John Spencer, the publisher of the 1640 edition of *A Mad World My Masters.*

I hope [he writes] the Reading thereof shall not prove distastefull unto any in particular, nor hurtfull unto any in generall; but I rather trust that the Language and the plot which you shall find in each Scene, shall rather be commended & applauded, than any way derided or scorned. In the action, which is the life of a Comedy, and the glory of the Author, it hath bin sufficiently expressed, to the liking of the Spectators, and commendations of the Actors; who have set it forth in such lively colours, and to the meaning of the Gentleman that true penn'd it, that I dare say few can excell them, though some may equall them. In the reading of one *Act* you ghesse the consequence, for here is no bumbasted or fustian stuffe; but every line weighed as with ballance; & every sentence placed with judgement and deliberation.[1]

The respect shown here for the orthodox academic point of view conflicts with our modern picture of the popular Elizabethan dramatists as splendidly unconcerned with contemporary text-book criticism. We have so far succeeded in suppressing the literary value of Elizabethan drama in our playhouses, that we find it hard to believe that Shakespeare, for instance, regarded his plays as poetry, and wrote them to provide a literary experience in the theatre, knowing that *actio* would reproduce for his audiences the variations of style in which he had expressed his creative imagining. For Shakespeare is often regarded as the opponent of the rhetorical acting described in the earlier chapters of this book. And those who take this view of him look for confirmation to the words addressed by Hamlet to the Players.[2] But the poet has put into the mouth of his Prince nothing that conflicts with the directions normally provided by the teachers of rhetorical delivery. Christopher Johnson wanted his boys to put into the voice 'a certain amount of elevation, depression and modulation'. Wright, too, was stressing the importance of speaking 'trippingly' when he insisted that 'flexibility of voice' is essential for the preservation of accent. All the authorities whom I have quoted in the first four chapters agree with Hamlet on

---

[1] Sigs. A3^r, A3^v.   [2] III. ii.

the importance of 'flexion' in the voice to avoid monotony and to
give both beauty and meaning to the words pronounced. Again,
they all insist as he does that the arms are to be moved with
grace and not thrown about violently. 'Nor do not saw the air
too much with your hand thus', says Hamlet, echoing innumer-
able others who must have made this observation since Quintilian first said disapprovingly, 'Solet esse et pigra et trepida
et secanti similis'[1]—'There are others, again, whose hands are
sluggish or tremulous or inclined to saw the air.' Hamlet's remark is not enough to justify our crediting Shakespeare with a
dislike of rhetorical gesture. For Bulwer, in a work written ex-
pressly in praise of that art, also warns his reader that 'To use
the action of one that Saws or Cuts; or of one dancing the
Pyrrique Gallyard; . . . are actions prevaricant in Rhetorick,
and condemned by *Quintilian*'.[2] If we could only have seen what
Burbage did as he said 'thus', we should know exactly what
Shakespeare objected to: but it is clear, I think, that it was not
the rhetorical use of the hand and arm as such. If we read the
modern 'slash' for the Elizabethan 'saw', we realize, too, that
Shakespeare, like Quintilian and Bulwer, wanted an elegant,
graceful movement of the arm instead of a harsh, ungraceful
slash. Discretion and moderation are the qualities valued in
oratory as well as by Hamlet. And as for the direction: 'Suit the
action to the word, the word to the action', it is but an echo of
Horatian teachings on decorum. 'The generall rule is, that the
gesture be correspondent to the ordering of the voice', says the
author of MS. Ashmole 768. We are told by Fraunce that gesture
'must follow the change and varietie of the voice, answering
thereunto in euerie respect'. And Bulwer bids us 'take care that
variety of gesture may answer the variety of voice and words'.
And again: 'Gesture must attend upon every flexion of the
voice.' Hamlet's words are repeated almost exactly by Heywood,
when he insisted that by appearing in plays the student at the
University became proficient in rhetorical gesture, learning 'to
fit his phrases to his action, and his actions to his phrase'. The

[1] Ed. cit., iv. 306–7.   [2] *Chiron.*, pp. 102–3.

argument was used again fifty years later in the dedication 'To all humours' placed before Clark's *Marciano*, a tragi-comedy printed at Edinburgh in 1663.

And we see even in our dayes, how all such as are educat in the Jesuit Schools, where no less then amongst publick Actors the Stage is dayly trod gain an unspotted reputation of compleat Orators throughout all the Christian world. And the defficiency (or rather wilfull contempt of this education) is the reason why many of our pretenders to wit, now a dayes forsooth, either whistle of a tedious harrangue with no more motion then a statue, or else use such a canting constrained tone, with such ridiculous grimassees, as they seem rather to imitate a Mountebanks Zany, in his apish gestures, then to aspire to the title of accomplished Orators. Whereas to deliver a speech naturally, that the action may sute the words, and the words the action; although dissonant to the pedantry of this age, . . . yet is, by the approbation of all the intelligent world, the chiefest ingredient of an ingenuous Orator.[1]

Clark insists that the only way to act 'naturally' is the way taught in the Jesuit schools, the way expounded by Bulwer and taught in the schools of pre-Restoration England. All who were accustomed to the perfection of this art would decry as 'unnatural' both the lack of 'motion' which is normal on our stage, and the 'canting constrained tone with ridiculous grimassees', which is denounced by Hamlet. For it is the imperfect rhetorical style to which he objects; and everything that he demands would be given by the good rhetorical actor of the time. When the Prince speaks of holding the mirror up to nature, he is describing the purpose, not the manner, of playing. Opera, too, can legitimately be described as holding up the mirror to nature, showing mankind its vices and its follies. In neither case is naturalistic acting essential to achieve this purpose. It is true that, if the acting is bad, the play is not effective in so far as human characteristics are not faithfully reproduced. But in Shakespeare's day these were reproduced by a stylized decorum, not by naturalistic imitation: and the whole tenor of these words to the Players is consistent with the doctrine of decorum

[1] W. Clark, *Marciano* (1663), pp. (4)–(5).

expounded by the teachers of rhetorical delivery and academic commentators on dramatic poetry.

What precisely any age, or any person, means by 'nature' as a quality of art, requires careful definition if it is not to be misunderstood. Too often 'natural' means very little more than 'in the manner which the speaker or writer has come to regard as normally correct'. To act 'naturally' in Shakespeare's time was no more to act naturalistically than to sing naturally in opera is to sing naturalistically. Gildon in his *Life of Betterton* reports that actor as stating that '*Nature*' is 'the Rule of just Acting'. But he adds that once this rule is accepted

the same Difficulty will arise here as in Writing, where all sides agree, that Nature is the sovereign Guide and Scope; but then they are not so agreed in what *Nature* is: the Skilful lay down those Signs, Marks, and Lineaments of *Nature*, that you may know when she is truly drawn, when not; the Unskilful, which is the greater and more noisy part, leave it so at large, that it amounts to no more, than every one's Fancy, . . . what pleases one, he calls Nature; what pleases another, that he calls Nature. . . . I instance this, to show that there seems a Necessity of some Marks, or Rules to fix the Standard of what is *Natural*, and what not, else it is a loose vague Word of no manner of Use or Authority.[1]

There is very little certainty that these are actually the words of Betterton, though I believe that they represent his views. It is most likely that, knowing Betterton's opinions, Gildon wrote an outline of acting and put it into the actor's mouth in this biography. The style of acting described here agrees in many details with Bulwer and other pre-Restoration writers on the subject. And in their day, which was also Shakespeare's, there existed well-known 'Marks, or Rules to fix the Standard of what is *Natural*'. According to modern convention the *actio* described by Bulwer is very unnatural: yet, as we have seen already, he insists that it is in conformity with 'Nature'. Nowhere is he more certain of this than in a passage at the beginning of *Chironomia*:

Nature exhorts all men to Action consentaneous to the stile of their Elocution: which inbred and commodious propensitie, unlesse

[1] C. Gildon, *Life of Mr. Thomas Betterton* (1710), p. 88.

illustrated by Art, and confirmed by exercitation, is, as *Trapezuntius* notes, but as a field untill'd, which runs wild with disorder'd productions. Art being the Imitator which perfects Nature, makes her actions more dilucid, illustrious and sweet, by her positive accommodations. For whatsoever Nature doth institute in the individuals worthy observation, reduced into one exact idea, built upon generall precepts, by a perpetuall order, Art doth expose under one aspect of the Understanding: and Nature againe placed by Art, beholds the excellent actions of eminent men, and expresses them by a happy exercitation.

He now adds, in a passage already quoted, that the ancient rhetoricians approved only of such gestures of the hand as had 'some similitude with the truth of Nature'.[1]

Hamlet's directions cannot be taken by themselves as reliable evidence for the style of acting of Shakespeare's or any other day. Modern writers on the theatre are in the habit of quoting them in support of the naturalistic and near-naturalistic acting of the modern stage. These directions have likewise been used in support of every style of acting known to the English theatre since the seventeenth century. In the early years of the eighteenth century Hamlet's words were interpreted in support of the rhetorical style of Betterton and Booth. Steele, in the well-known note in No. 35 of *The Tatler*, reprints this 'Abstract of the Laws of Action'. He found these fulfilled in the acting of Betterton, he tells us in two other papers:[2] and in yet another he deplores that among the clergy of Britain 'this Art of Speaking, with the proper Ornaments of Voice and Gesture is wholly neglected'.[3] Gildon, too, in the work to which I have already referred, takes Hamlet's words as proof of Shakespeare's approval of rhetorical action when performed correctly. I think it is clear that in the early eighteenth century whoever adhered strictly to the rhetorical style was considered to be acting 'naturally'; whilst to break the rules of this style was to be 'unnatural'. If we do not see this clearly we shall inevitably find

---

[1] *Chiron.*, pp. 20–1.
[2] No. 71 and No. 167.
[3] No. 66.

ourselves in the predicament of Malone, who wrote: 'I have never been able to meet with any person who had seen Betterton or Booth; but am persuaded that their manner was very pompous and false, and that they spoke in a high, unnatural tone. Yet if we are to believe the *Tatler*'s description of Betterton's Hamlet, it was all nature.'[1]

Hamlet's advice to the players, then, cannot be taken as an attack on the art which I have outlined in my earlier chapters, but rather as the reverse. Yet, it may be argued, there are passages in Shakespeare which strike us as too realistic for the rhetorical style of acting. Was the performance of these rhetorical? No certain answer can be given. It is obvious that the style must have varied not only from theatre to theatre, but also according to the needs of individual scenes. Nevertheless, the fact that a scene strikes us as realistic to-day does not mean that the style of its first performances was necessarily realistic in the realism of to-day. This becomes clear as soon as we consider the case of Molière, whose comedies are superficially as realistic as any scene in Shakespeare, if not more so: yet the French comedians who first performed them acted in nothing like the modern realistic style. What seems real is not necessarily realistic, as we are repeatedly reminded every time we go to the cinema. Garrick's name has come down to us as a byword for realism; and yet he acted Macbeth in the coat of an eighteenth-century gentleman.

That Elizabethan acting varied in accordance with the style of the words to be spoken is, I believe, something that we can be permitted to state without fear of contradiction. That is what Shakespeare tells us with his 'suit the action to the word', and it is what Bulwer says with his 'Nature exhorts all men to Action consentaneous to the stile of their Elocution'. For what the performer did was determined in advance by the dramatist's words. What distinguished one character from another on the stage was the result of the 'elocution' of the lines provided by the author. And given two actors of equal talent, each would be able to

[1] Sir J. Prior, *Life of Edmond Malone* (1860), p. 345.

perform the same speech in exactly the same way, apart from differences of voice and personal appearance.

That there was a generally accepted body of rules as to what was a fault, what a virtue, seems to be indicated by the Elizabethan custom of acting for wagers. In Shakespeare's day there were people prepared to risk their money backing one player to act against another; and it is unlikely that anyone would be prepared to accept the arbitrary taste of the judges where money was involved. According to the *Henslowe Papers* a certain 'W. P.' accepted a wager from 'a party affected to other actors' and backed Edward Alleyn to outshine them in any play in which Bentley or Knell had appeared.[1] In *Ratseis Ghost* (1605) Ratsey urges a likely actor to leave the countryside for London: 'I durst venture all the money in my purse on thy head, to play Hamlet with him [Burbage] for a wager.'[2] Dekker, in his *Jests to Make You Merry* (1607), tells of a 'Paire of Players growing into an emulous contention of one anothers worth, refusde to put themselues to a day of hearing (as any Players would have done) but stood onely vpon their good parts'.[3] And in his *Gull's Hornbook* (1609) Dekker, ending his chapter *How a gallant should behaue himselfe in a Tauerne*, says 'let any hooke draw you either to a Fencers supper, or to a Players that acts such a part for a wager'.[4] There was also the case of William Fennor, who, as Sir Edmund Chambers tells us, 'in the course of a rhyming controversy with John Taylor, makes the following boast of his histrionic talent:

> And let me tell thee this to calme thy rage,
> I chaleng'd Kendall on the Fortune stage;
> And he did promise 'fore an audience,
> For to oppose me.'[5]

Acting for wagers is also mentioned in the Epilogue to *The Jew of Malta*, printed in the edition of 1633, and spoken at the Cockpit by William Perkins, who acted Barabas:

> Nor think that this day any prize was plaid,
> Here were no betts at all, no wagers laid.[6]

[1] Ed. W. W. Greg, p. 32.   [2] Sig. B1ʳ.   [3] Sig. B4ʳ.
[4] Sig. F2ᵛ.   [5] *The Elizabethan Stage*, ii. 191.   [6] Sig. A4ᵛ.

And it seems that amateurs may have taken part in the same practice, if we are justified in taking seriously the Citizen's boast in *The Knight of the Burning Pestle* (Prologue), that Ralph

> should have plaid *Jeronimo*
> With a shoo-maker for a wager.

All the evidence goes to show that rhetorical acting on the stage was conducted according to an accepted body of rules. The actor's function was not to 'create', but to perform. He was to use his voice and body to give life to the text: 'Player is like a garment which the Tailor maketh at the direction of the owner: so they frame their action, at the disposing of the Poet.'[1] And again, 'Plaier was euer the life of dead poesie'.[2] So long as this was the player's part, and so long as he was trained to communicate the variations of thought and emotion composed into words by the author, so long was the audience's response in the theatre a response to a literary experience and so long could the dramatist be confident that what he wrote as poetry would be performed none the less as drama. In the theatre, as in the study, the poet's words are all that count. From them alone is it possible to create his play over again. And in the Elizabethan theatre, if Heywood is to be believed—and all the evidence suggests that he is to be believed—rhetorical acting could provide the audience with an experience as intense as anything we are likely to know to-day.

To turne to our domesticke hystories, what English blood seeing the person of any bold English man presented and doth not hugge his fame, . . . pursuing him in his enterprise with his best wishes, and as beeing wrapt in contemplation, offers to him in his hart all prosperous performance, as if the Personator were the man Personated, so bewitching a thing is liuely and well spirited action, that it hath power to new mold the harts of the spectators and fashion them to the shape of any noble and notable attempt.[3]

[1] T. Gainsford, *The Rich Cabinet* (1616), sigs. Q5^v–Q6^r.
[2] Ibid., sig. Q4^r.   [3] Op. cit., sig. B4^r.

INDEX OF PERSONS, PLACES, AND WORKS

INDEX OF SUBJECTS

PRINTED IN
GREAT BRITAIN
AT THE
UNIVERSITY PRESS
OXFORD
BY
CHARLES BATEY
PRINTER
TO THE
UNIVERSITY